TRIATHLON

TRIATHLON

A COMPLETE GUIDE TO MULTI-SPORT SUCCESS

Karin Zeitvogel

SBL Springfield Books Limited

© Karin Zeitvogel 1994

This edition first published by Springfield Books Limited, Norman Road, Denby Dale, Huddersfield HD8 8TH, West Yorkshire, England

First edition 1994

British Library Cataloguing in Publication Data

Zeitvogel, Karin
    Triathlon
    I Title
    796

Cased   ISBN: 1 85688 032 X
Paperback ISBN: 1 85688 045 1

Design and illustrations: Chris Hand, Design for Print
Typesetting: Paragon Typesetters, Queensferry, Clwyd
Printed and bound in Hong Kong by Colorcraft Ltd

Dedication
To Gilles

Photo credits
The author and publishers wish to thank the following people:
Richard Graham for the photographs on pages 16, 22, 23, 35, 53, 54, 60 (both), 69, 72, 73, 75, 79, 80, 81, 82, 83, 89, 98, 100 (right), 104, 108, 125, 126 (upper); Photosport International for the photographs on the cover, frontis and pages 40, 42, 61, 86, 94, 99 (both), 100 (left), 136, 149; Sporting Pictures for the photographs on pages 8, 31, 57, 62 (both), 64, 66, 85, 101, 129, 143; Professional Sport for the photograph on pages 17, 18, 36, 71, 74, 76; Jean-Luc Petit for the photographs on pages 90, 121, 122, 124, 126 (lower); Gilles Trousselier for the photographs on pages 25, 26, 59 (left), 63; Stewart Clarke for the photograph on page 140; Charles Pineau for the photograph on page 50; Philippe Roman for the photograph on page 144. All other photography is by Karin Zeitvogel

Acknowledgements
The author and publishers would like to thank the following contributors for their generous help in the production of this book:
Dr Sarah Springman; Lennard Zinn; Dr Domhnall MacAuley; The British Triathlon Association for the *Competitor information* on pages 150–157

Jacket photography
Front: images from the 1992 Bath Triathlon, Britain's biggest event. Although the previous day's heavy rain created problems with debris in the water, the 1500m swim, 40km bike and 10km run was won by Holland's Rob Barel
Back: ecstatic Alison Hamilton of Ireland won the women's triathlon in Bath
Frontis: competitors at the start of the Bath Triathlon, one of Britain's largest events, make a last minute reconnoitre of the swim course, adjusting caps and goggles to prepare for the mêlée

Contents

Preface

Sarah Springman lives her life at 100 miles per hour, balancing mundane chores with her work at Cambridge University, her tireless efforts for triathlon, her personal commitments and her training. Sarah has amassed 11 British titles, plus two European Ironman-distance titles. She is Vice-President of the International Triathlon Union and is partly responsible for securing the 1993 World Championships for Manchester. At 37, she still competes in triathlon too.

In fact, my own triathlon 'career', as Springman describes these things, wouldn't have been possible without her. I took my initial steps in triathlon in 1984, when I attended her first ever women's triathlon training camp at the Bognor Regis Butlin's holiday camp. We shared the centre that weekend with a clown convention and some religious fanatics. Or maybe both lots were just other groups of triathletes.

In 1987, she embroiled me even deeper, when she asked me to be her support team at the European Ironman championships in Finland. Sarah Springman was well on her way to winning when bad luck struck: a slow puncture and a tubular tyre that wouldn't come off the rim cost her a good eight minutes on the bike section. She lost the race by four minutes. But she didn't complain afterwards. She congratulated the winner, Sarah Coope, and took her own personal disappointment home with her.

I remember with pride how one New Year's Day, Springman joined me and a group of cyclists in a 50-mile reliability ride. Coming down off the Hog's Back near Guildford, Surrey, I knew that after a sharp left-hand turn, the hammer was going to come down as we rode up the A3. Springman got there first, and I was on her wheel. I hung on for a couple of miles, with her turning to look occasionally, and still seeing this obstinate friend of hers who had no right to be hanging on the wheel of one of the best women cyclists in Britain. I went off the back when I laughed at the improbable scenario.

When I asked her for advice and for help with this book, she willingly gave it. The following pages contain advice and tips from one of the best triathletes Britain has known. For example, to improve her swimming technique Sarah thinks about dolphins and uses them in swimming visualisation exercises, even donning a pair of flippers every now and again and butterfly kicking to the end of the pool. There's nothing to stop you from doing the same thing and Sarah is sure it has helped her and made her training more fun: to a large extent that is what it's about.

To Sarah, thanks for the help with this book and for getting me involved in the first place, and for those of you reading this, remember: triathlon should be fun.

Introduction

Your first triathlon is like your first kiss. You never forget it; it becomes a benchmark against which you can measure all that follow, and no matter how much you exaggerate it to your friends, they'll hang on your every word as you recount it to them.

On the other hand, if first triathlons and kisses were comparable in every way, I wouldn't have been so keen to corner Richard Cassilly on the train platform for my second kiss. My first triathlon was difficult, and attempted in circumstances any being of sound mind and body wouldn't have entertained for an instant. It was the 1986 London Triathlon, an Olympic distance event of 1500 metres (0.9 miles) swimming, 40 kilometres (25 miles) cycling and 10 kilometres (6.25 miles) running. I was recovering from flu, I'd put in too many hours at work but I lined up at the start line regardless.

At the sound of the claxon I jumped into the waters of the Thames' Royal Docks in East London along with 399 other triathletes. My lungs constricted with the chill. These were, after all, pre-wetsuit days, the epoch in triathlon where body fat was acceptable because it helped to keep you warm in water of 16 degrees Celsius.

I started to swim a combination of front crawl, breast- and backstroke, the latter being employed because rolling onto my back was the only way I could breathe. Every once in awhile, waves of grease and used car parts would envelope us. After far too long in those filthy conditions, I left the water and headed for my bike.

I had a Peugeot triathlon bike, which my friends and I thought was **the** business. It was made of Reynolds 501 tubing, had ordinary drop bars, non-indexed gears (they didn't exist yet) and spoked 700C wheels. There was another Peugeot bike on the market at the time, which was blue instead of white like mine; it didn't have the swim-bike-run figures prancing along its top tube, and only had one bottle cage (we triathletes were given two). Also made of 501 tubing, that bike was essentially the same as my bike, but it cost about £20 less.

In those days you had to look hard to see if someone was riding a triathlon bike: today, the differences are immediately obvious. Triathlon has substantially influenced the bike market and after being scorned by traditional cyclists for years is now accepted as a source of innovation. In fact, when Greg LeMond won the Tour de France in 1989 beating Laurent Fignon by eight seconds, the American attributed

Triathlon was included in the Commonwealth Games in 1990. It will make its debut in the Atlanta Olympics in 1996

his success to triathlon bars.

I pedalled around the streets of Beckton, feeling nauseous from swallowing too much Thames water, but overtaking a lot of people. After five or six laps of the bike course, I returned to the transition area, dismounted, chucked my leather strip helmet on the ground (there were no rules regarding hardshell helmets then) and ran off for the ten-kilometre run. Halfway through I started to show classic signs of dehydration followed by signs of the bonk: everything slowed down, the glycogen in my muscles had been replaced by air, and a little voice in my head was saying, 'Sit down . . .'

Another little voice was telling me

that I had to finish this first triathlon, and I did. Someone handed me a packet of dextrose tablets, which got me through about 400 metres at a time before their instant kick was replaced by a plummet in blood sugar. Today, that same helpful soul would probably hand me a PowerBar, but they didn't exist then either.

So that was my first triathlon, and after an experience like that, you would think I'd have stuck to tiddlywinks. But I knew I could do better. I set about training intelligently and two months later tried my second triathlon, with better results: I was seventh woman out of the water, second woman after the bike, and fourth after the run. That, I thought, was more like it. I now enjoy being a healthy recreational triathlete.

Since the early days triathlon has evolved into a high-tech, mature sport, and has become a way of life for those who practise it. Now is probably the best time to be entering triathlon: there is a wealth of new technology around to help you improve your performance safely. The sport is open to people from every walk of life, you can compete at every level from beginner to professional, and the people who practise it will welcome you to their sport. Triathlon is exciting and healthy, and if you approach it in the right way you can't help but win your own swim, bike and run battles.

CHAPTER 1

A brief history of triathlon

Triathlon took on legendary status almost as soon as it was born – after all this was a sport practised by men and women who, compared to your everyday couch potato, were demigods. They were suntanned, they had body fat percentages in the single digits, when they wore Lycra, there were no lumps. This was a sport that required something extraordinary of those who attempted it. This was not a sport that could have evolved slowly and calmly, like tennis or badminton. Triathlon, the media claimed, had a fiery birth, a naissance that immediately classed it apart from other sports, a conception fertilised by minds that beat to a different drum.

In reality, triathlon did just evolve slowly and steadily from the healthy way of life in southern California. To be precise it was in the triathlon mecca of San Diego that the sport first started. In the early '70s, a San Diegan, appropriately named David Pain, celebrated his birthday by holding the David Pain Birthday Biathlon. Competitors ran 6.2 miles and then swam half a mile.

In 1974, the idea of David Pain's Birthday Biathlon was extended, when two more San Diegans organised an event called the Mission Bay Triathlon. That first triathlon, whose founders Don Shannahan and Jack Johnstone should be mentioned here so that their names can pass, along with Pain's, into the annals of triathlon history, encompassed a 2.8-mile run, a five-mile bike ride, a quarter-mile swim, another two-mile run and then **another** quarter-mile swim. Thankfully, the formula for triathlons has been simplified since then.

That first event was something of a haphazard affair. There were no bike racks, no race numbers, no tents where masseurs' hands soothed weary competitors at the end of the race. Such was the inauspicious start of triathlon.

In spite of the fact that triathlon was up and running, swimming and cycling in San Diego for years beforehand, a lot of people still think that the sport started with the birth of the Hawaii Ironman in 1978. Granted, the history of Ironman is a romantic one. After a beer-inspired argument over who is the fittest – a swimmer, a cyclist or a runner – and who has the better endurance – the younger or the older athlete – John Collins, a US Navy commander stationed in Hawaii, proposed a unique, if slightly mad, challenge. In a single day, competitors would combine three already existing races into one event: the Waikiki Rough Water Swim, the Around Oahu Bike Race and the Honolulu Marathon. And so on 18 February 1978, 15 slightly mad men gathered on the sands of Waikiki Beach. They gathered there early in the morning, because usually you can't move on Waikiki Beach for all of the prostrate holiday-makers. The first of 12 finishers crossed the finish line after 11 hours and 46 minutes, and for his efforts, Gordon Haller, a taxi driver, received a hand-brazed trophy in the shape of a man, with a metal pipe for his body and a nut for his head.

If Haller were to win the Ironman today, he would receive a huge cheque. But Haller's time in 1978 would probably not even earn him an age-group victory these days.

Just as 1972 saw the birth of triathlon and 1978 the birth of Ironman, 1982 was the year in which triathlon really came under the media

spotlight. Again, it was the Ironman which prompted the hullaballoo: on 6 February, 1982, a petite freckle-faced Californian named Julie Moss collapsed while leading the women's race, with only footsteps needed to cross the finish line. As Moss made a superhuman effort to finish the race, her closest rival, Kathleen McCartney, passed her, taking top honours by just 29 seconds.

Moss' ordeal was projected into living rooms around the world on ABC television's *Wide World of Sport*, which on a Saturday afternoon can attract and hold the attention of more viewers than the combined populations of Switzerland, Sweden, Norway and Finland. Moss' grit and determination inspired thousands of athletes to take up the Ironman challenge, and when the next Hawaii Ironman was held just six months later, the number of entrants had jumped from 580 to 850.

Among competitors in the October 1982 race was a newcomer to the Ironman, Mark Allen. He was, by his own admission, inspired by seeing Moss on television to pit himself against the rigours of this classic triathlon. Allen dropped out of his first Ironman attempt because of mechanical difficulties with his bike. After further unsuccessful attempts at Ironman, Allen finally found his winning form in 1989, when he dethroned Ironman legend, Dave Scott, who has won the race six times. Allen also set a new course record in 1989, of 8.09:15. He has won every year since then. Incidentally, he subsequently married Julie Moss.

The Ironman still captures the imaginations of armchair athletes around the world and continues to inspire its competitors. But swimming 2.4 miles, cycling 112 miles and then running a marathon isn't the only formula for triathlon. In fact, the most popular is what is called the Olympic distance: 1500 metres (0.9 miles) in the water, 40km (25 miles) on the bike and a 10km (6.25miles) run. This became the basis for the first official triathlon world championships held in 1989, in Avignon, France.

Before that, as with many young sports, there had been unofficial world championships all over the place. But Avignon was the first to be sanctioned by the International Triathlon Union (ITU), a world governing body whose mature outlook has helped triathlon to progress markedly during its short existence.

The French were perfect hosts during the memorable Avignon World Championships. Avignon, famous for its 'pont' that stretches only halfway over the Rhone, its Palais des Papes, in which a victorious Mark Allen and New Zealand's Erin Baker gave glowing speeches, the plane-tree lined transition and finish area, was the perfect setting.

Triathletes from 38 countries set off on the swim, and it was New Zealand's Richard Wells who hit land first. Behind him, Glenn Cook of Great Britain and the United States' Garrett McCarthy ran to their bikes, stripping off wetsuits *en route*. Neither Cook nor Wells had enjoyed their best season so far, but their results in Avignon – Cook came second and Wells third – set the record straight and delighted their fans.

The following year, the ITU World Championships were held at Disneyworld in Florida, the year after on Australia's Gold Coast in 1992 in Muskoka, in Canada and in Manchester, England, in 1993. The hemisphere-hopping is deliberate and reflects triathlon's global outlook.

As triathlon continues to mature, its history becomes richer and its races more widespread: today, you can compete in triathlons from Senegal to Surrey, from Reunion Island in the Indian Ocean to Roth in West Germany. There are European Triathlon Union (ETU) and International Triathlon Union and national series. A number of triathletes make their living doing nothing but swimming, cycling and running and for some of them, the sport pays very well.

The names of the triathletes filling the top slot on the podiums at the sport's prestigious races changes constantly – and yet the legends refuse to die. Mark Allen won the Ironman again in 1992, breaking the record he set in 1985 by seven seconds. The women's record too reached new levels as Paula Newby-Fraser took her fifth Ironman victory. Glenn Cook won the European Middle Distance title in Finland, while Briton Simon Lessing fulfilled promise he had shown in earlier years when he ran away with the win in Muskoka. Another Briton,

Spencer Smith, took the junior title, with Australia's Michellie Jones and Germany's Sonia Krolik, the first senior and junior women respectively. In 1993 Smith took his second consecutive world title, albeit this time as a senior; Michellie Jones sprinted to her second consecutive world title after a tough battle with America's Karen Smyers.

And thanks to the lobbying and tireless groundwork of the behind the scenes people in triathlon – such as ITU President Les McDonald – the likelihood of triathlon becoming an Olympic sport is growing all the time.

That's a far cry from the days of Pain in San Diego, 1972.

Sarah remembers the start of triathlon

In June 1983, I read an article about triathlon in a magazine. It wasn't a triathlon magazine – I don't think they existed in Britain yet – but the article was very nicely laid out and featured a picture of Allison Roe wearing a tinpot helmet and riding a bike. Allison was a star marathon runner – about 2:27-ish – from New Zealand.

The piece grabbed my attention, and when I learned that there was a triathlon scheduled for six weeks' time in Reading – a 1200-metre swim, 35-mile bike ride and a half marathon – I got down to the business of training. I knew I could run a half marathon, because I'd done many of those before. But I was a little daunted by the idea of the swim, because I was incapable of swimming front crawl for three, 27-yard pool-lengths, and we would be swimming over ten times that distance in open water.

There were a lot of people at that race who, like me, had never done a triathlon before. Nobody wore wetsuits. People didn't know about things like goggles misting up, about swimming on other people's feet. Having worked as hard as I could in six weeks on my swimming, I managed to maintain a semblance of front crawl all the way. And then came the biking section.

This was another voyage of self-discovery. I'd never sat on a bike for 35 miles non-stop before. I'd borrowed a bike – too large for me, and extremely heavy – from a friend and got about a fortnight's training in before the race. I hadn't a clue what I needed to do with the gears so I chose the biggest and hardest, and I don't think that helped me much.

The bikes we rode back then had normal racing handlebars. Some people in the race had mudguards. Nobody had tri-shorts, HED wheels or anything of that nature. That was very far into the future.

I was passed by a lot of people on the bike. (God knows how I finished the swim in front of them, but I did.) Most of the people had an encouraging word as they whizzed past. There was tremendous camaraderie because this was, for all of us, a great journey into the unknown.

After the bike there was a long run, which seemed to be the tendency in triathlon in those days. Many competitors had a lot of running experience, and early triathlons favoured them. I was passed by Chrissie Barrett, she of 100-mile and 24-hour run fame, who had finished the Hawaii Ironman the year before. She was a tremendous runner, but hated swimming and wasn't desperately interested in biking. Julia Kendall of the British

Britain's women have shone in triathlon since the early days of the sport. Here, Sarah Coope – whom the French refer to as *la jolie Anglaise*, or the pretty Englishwoman – makes the transition from the swim to the bike section in the 1988 Nice Triathlon, in which she finished third

women's modern pentathlon team won that race. Josie May, who won the first British National Championships ahead of me later that same season was second. Chrissie Barrett finished third, I was fourth, and Caron Groves fifth.

The next big development in my triathlon career came after an all-night party. The friends throwing the party had insisted that I come, and I said I would, if I could drink only orange juice. Of course, faced with champagne, my resolve crumbled, and after drinking far too much and getting only one hour's sleep, I met up with Caron Groves and we drove to the race. That is, Caron drove. I was still under the influence.

The race was on an airfield in Portsmouth. It was windy, hot and I was very dehydrated. I don't know how I did it, but I finished ahead of Caron and won my first triathlon. It was my first and only triathlon victory

under the influence of alcohol.

Next stop: the National Championships at Kielder Water. It was supposed to be a mile swim (but it was considerably longer), 60 miles on the bike and 17 miles of running. Standard distances were still a thing of the future.

The swim was extremely cold, and a number of us got hypothermia. Caron Groves nearly drowned and had to be rescued by some other swimmers. Josie May, who was a superb swimmer, belted off at high speed and was gone by miles. I managed to head off at 90 degrees to the direction I should have been going and had to be battered on the head by a canoeist to get me back on course.

When I came out of the water, I was confronted by what looked like a refugee camp. There were people lying everywhere, packed into the only shelter – a tiny hut – with heating. I was shaking so much I

A young Glen Cook runs to victory in the Prince's Triathlon, West London, 1985. The event has long since passed but Cook still runs to victory

could hardly change into my cycling gear. And during the swim, something had got into my goggles and irritated my eye, so I could only see out of one eye. You try riding down whacking great hills against a strong headwind, one eye screaming in pain and the other screaming in sympathy . . . a 90 degree bend in the road and lots of black and white arrows trying to tell you which way to go, but just succeeding at confusing you. Life was pretty interesting in those days.

I was so cold going into the bike ride, it took me about 20 miles before I stopped shivering. The run wasn't much better: I tripped over something and fell flat on my face. Still, I finished second, behind Josie.

The final race of that first year of my triathlon career was in Nice at the unofficial world championships. It was all very glitzy. There were lots of Americans, lots of 'famous' people whom I'd heard about. Superstars.

Julia Kendall was very much favoured to finish best British woman. I caught her on the first climb on the bike, and thought, 'Wow – I'm the first Brit now.' I carried on at a good rate and descended quite well. It was tremendously exhilarating climbing in the hills around Nice, and all the way through we had wonderful support from everyone: the police, people out on their bikes to watch the race, everyone.

Alas there was a problem of drafting, even in those early days of triathlon. I saw a couple of people being met by friends at the

14

beginning of a climb, and they'd draft them all the way up to the top!

After the run I found myself in eighth place. America's Colleen Cannon won the women's race; and Mark Allen started his incredible winning streak at the Nice Triathlon that year by taking the men's title for the second year running. I felt as if I too had achieved something after Nice. It was the first time I'd done an event of international standing, and I'd finished top European woman. That made me think that, if I trained a little harder and learned a bit more about this amazing sport, I might improve.

Paula Newby-Fraser holds the women's record for the Ironman and is now internationally recognised as one of the world's outstanding female athletes. When she first started in triathlon she was regularly beaten by Sarah Springman

Right: in the early days of triathlon, Springman raced for the Freewheel line-up. She sported a trendy tri-suit and the latest in disk wheels

Mark Allen is one of the sport's most formidable and enduring competitors. One of triathlon's original Big Four – along with Dave Scott, Scott Tinley and Scott Molina – Allen has won the Nice Triathlon ten times and the Hawaii Ironman more times consecutively than any other triathlete. He is shown here scoring his eighth Nice win, in 1991

CHAPTER 2

The first step

If you've decided that you want to give triathlon a try, or you feel that you can improve as a triathlete, the next step is to train. If, like Sarah, you want to make the most of your potential as a triathlete, then you have to set about training intelligently.

First of all decide to listen selectively to the advice that your friends, clubmates and everyone else will offer. They will undoubtedly tell you what worked for them; listen to what they say, but keep an open mind, and remember that it might not work for you.

The training programme you finally opt for should be tailor-made for you, and you should be instrumental in its design. Start by asking yourself a few questions:

1 How ambitious are you? Do you want to be an internationally ranked professional or do you simply want to make it through an Olympic distance – 1500 metre swim,

40km bike, 10km run – triathlon?

2 How much time can you realistically devote to triathlon? If the answer to number one above is that you want to be an internationally ranked pro, then the answer to this question had better be, 'a lot'.

3 What are your strengths? Are you a top-flight swimmer? Did you grow up running 10 kilometres with Liz McColgan? Or have you never even swung a leg over a bike? If you have a good basic level of fitness, you'll be able to start your training programme at a more advanced stage than that of an absolute beginner.

Now ask yourself another set of questions:

1 What distance of triathlon do you want to concentrate on? You may want to set as your goal as an Ironman-distance race in a year's time. If that's the case, then you'll need to do a lot of distance training – the Ironman covers 2.4 miles in the water, 112 miles on the bike and 26.2 miles running. A

middle distance or long course triathlon is half these distances, and is sometimes referred to as a half-Ironman. The most popular format for triathlon is held over the so-called Olympic distance: 1500 metres swimming, 40 km cycling and 10km running.

2 How often can you train?

3 How often should you train?

Numbers two and three might seem very similar in theory, but in practice they are miles apart. You might be able to include three, even four training sessions in a day, but if you are working, if you have a family, if you find that training three times a day without sufficient opportunity for rest between sessions is resulting in you being an anti-social, gaunt wreck, then you must re-assess your training. Often, you will gain more from undertraining than overtraining.

Now look at the race calendar (available from the National Governing Bodies of triathlon around the world) and choose the race or races you want to do in the next year. While you're planning your race calendar, bear in mind your own limitations as an athlete. Do you recover easily from strenuous efforts? If so, then you can probably afford to pencil in more events than the athlete who finds him or herself shattered after a five kilometre training run. Also remember that events such as the Hawaii Ironman or the ITU World Championships require you to successfully complete a qualifying event. Check out the races you want to do: your best source of information is the governing body for the sport.

Generally speaking, we can all recover sufficiently between races to put in a reasonable effort every six weeks. This doesn't mean that, physical limitations aside, you can't race every weekend. Just don't expect every race to produce a new personal best. When top athletes plan their yearly programmes, they select carefully the races they want to peak for: the World Championships, their country's national championships, a big money race, a race with great prestige. They may have races every weekend in between these events, but those races will be considered training runs, and their programmes will be based around the big events they have focused on.

CHAPTER 3

Food, glorious food

Food is a subject dear to every triathlete's heart. Many are amazed at how the triple sport allows them to consume food like a vacuum cleaner consumes dust. As a triathlete, you can increase your caloric intake without piling on the pounds, but you should be selective about what you eat.

If we divide comestibles into carbohydrate, protein and fat, then you should try to eat between 60–75% of your daily calories in the form of carbohydrate, 10–15% in the form of protein, and 10–30% in the form of fat. To help you to achieve this – although I don't think it was solely with triathletes in mind – manufacturers have started labelling foods. If you know that fat contains roughly nine calories per gramme, then, if a foodstuff's label gives you sufficient information (grammes of fat per 100 grammes and calories per 100 grammes) you should be able to calculate the percentage of calories you will be deriving from fat by eating a certain food. Carbohydrate and protein contain around four calories per gramme. If you were tempted to indulge in a vanilla mousse, you would see from the manufacturer's information that it contains about five grammes of fat and 141 Calories per 100 grammes. As there are about nine Calories in a gramme of fat, you can work out that around 45 Calories in a 100g serving of your mousse come from fat, or 32% (42 ÷ 14). You should really put the mousse back on the shelf and go buy a PowerBar.

Rather than walking around the supermarket with a calculator, learn to recognise which foods are rich in carbohydrate and should make up the bulk of your diet, and which are high in fat and should be approached with caution. As a rule of thumb, put foods with more than 10 grammes of fat per 100 grammes back on the shelf.

If you consume a balanced and

varied diet, you should be getting adequate carbohydrate, fat and protein.

Foods high in carbohydrate are: bread, pasta, rice, porridge, cereals, dried fruit, fresh fruit, chestnuts, beans, lentils, peas, potatoes.

Foods high in fat are: oils, butter and margarine (81%!), red meat, chicken if cooked with skin, duck, avocados, olives, nuts, full-fat dairy products, eg cheese, chocolate.

Keeping well hydrated should be one of your top priorities on the bike: Erin Baker shows you how

Why carbohydrate?

Carbohydrate is the main source of energy in our diet, but we can only use it to serve our energy needs once we have converted it into glucose, a simple sugar or monosaccharide. All carbohydrates are converted eventually into glucose for transport in the blood and for utilisation by the cells of the body. The glucose in our bloodstream is called upon to serve immediate energy needs.

We also store carbohydrate as glycogen, a polysaccharide or complex carbohydrate, in the muscles and liver. When more glucose than can be immediately metabolised enters the bloodstream, a healthy person will combine up to 30,000 glucose molecules to form glycogen. Then, when a need for glucose arises, the glycogen will be broken down.

Twice as much glycogen is stored in the muscles as in the liver. Liver glycogen is more readily available for replenishing blood sugar, while muscle glycogen is used primarily as fuel for the muscles. By ensuring that your diet is high in carbohydrate, you can store enough glycogen to see you through approximately two hours of activity, although this will vary from person to person.

Too little carbohydrate and you will suffer abnormal fat metabolism, breakdown of body protein (muscle), increased sodium excretion, loss of energy and fatigue – none of which is desirable for triathletes.

Why not fat?

Fat provides the human body with concentrated energy (remember, it has double the number of calories per gramme than carbohydrate) and helps to transport fat soluble vitamins in the body – vitamins A, D, E and K.

The problem is that, since the Second World War, westerners have steadily increased their fat intake. Some westerners consume close to 50% of their calories in fat.

This increases the risk of obesity as there is a parallel increase in percentage of calories consumed, and the susceptibility to heart and circulatory diseases, as high fat consumption can result in elevated cholesterol and triglyceride levels in the blood. There are exceptions to this rule: Eskimos, for instance, have a diet high in fat but suffer little or no heart disease. Their diet is, however, low in saturated fat, free from dairy products, and consists almost exclusively of fish.

As a triathlete, too much fat will slow you down by giving you extra weight to carry. And if you have high levels of cholesterol or triglycerides in the blood, then they could inhibit oxygen transport to your working muscles. In addition, fat takes a long time to digest – the reason a high fat meal gives you that satisfied feeling – so eating it before a race (if you want to take advantage of those concentrated calories) only results in a heavy feeling in the stomach. Remember, energy is of no use to you in its potential state: it has to be broken down and absorbed by the body first.

The importance of protein

The name protein comes from Greek and means 'of first importance'. Proteins have been called building blocks, the fundamental structural element of every cell in the body. Protein is used in the formation of new cartilage cells and for the lengthening of bone before calcification occurs. It is, therefore, essential that triathletes consume adequate protein by eating a balanced diet.

We need protein to supply essential amino acids, necessary for tissue growth and maintenance. The essential amino acids cannot be synthesized by

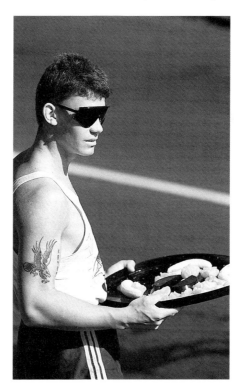

A feed-station volunteer offers competitors a choice of bananas or oranges, or bananas or oranges

the body, and therefore must be ingested. We also need protein to fulfil our requirement for nitrogen. You are in nitrogen equilibrium when your nitrogen intake from protein equals the nitrogen lost via excretion. All proteins are made up of nitrogen-containing compounds, the amino acids.

If you consume too much protein, you will store the excess as fat, and, as each gramme of protein produces the equivalent of 1.25 calories of unused energy, which is excreted via the urine as nitrogenous compounds, you will be also placing an unnecessary strain on your kidneys and other organs of excretion.

Try to keep your protein intake at around 15% of total calories. Sometimes, after a hard race, there may be justification to increase protein intake slightly to aid in recovery, but not over a prolonged period of time. Your body will probably give you signals as to what it wants and needs after a long race. Generally speaking, I steer clear of meat, but after competing in a 140km running race, which took in seven peaks of over 2000 metres, I had an uncanny craving for red meat. So too does Sarah Springman after the Ironman. These cravings might seem odd for a vegetarian but go for it – your body is telling you what it needs.

Good sources of protein are: skimmed milk and low-fat yogurt, soya products, Bovril, fish, lean meat, poultry, game, almonds and peanuts (but beware the high fat content in the latter).

Race food

If your daily diet is high in carbohydrate, then you should have no need to modify your eating habits before a race. By eating a high carbohydrate diet all of the time, you are, effectively, permanently carbo-loading.

During a race, remember that you have about two hours of stored energy in your liver and muscles in the form of glycogen. You can augment this energy, if need be – for example, during a half-Ironman or Ironman distance race – by ingesting carbohydrate during the race.

To illustrate this, look at the case of Joe and Sally. Joe and Sally are two dogs who ran for four to six hours before running out of energy. That was without taking in carbohydrate. When they consumed carbohydrate during their effort, they were able to run for 17 to 23 hours.

You may not show the same remarkable results as Joe or Sally, but you can postpone the point at which fatigue occurs, ie the point at which you run out of glycogen. If you eat carbohydrate during a race, glucose will be absorbed from your gut, and liver glycogen, which is released into the bloodstream when called upon, will be spared. The best way to take in carbohydrate during a race is to drink one of the sports drinks on the market. Prepare the drink according to the manufacturer's instructions – you don't want too concentrated a mix, as that will inhibit absorption by the gut.

Britain's Jack Maitland heads out on the run in the St Denis Triathlon on Reunion Island, grabbing a bottle of water on the way

The ideal mix is a five to eight percent carbohydrate content, which is usually what the manufacturers' instructions suggest.

While, generally speaking, you can get through an Olympic distance triathlon on stored energy and a sports drink, during longer triathlons, you would be advised to eat solids during the race. The obvious time to eat is on the bike, but you can also learn to eat while running.

Choose high carbohydrate, low-fat foods to eat during the race, but always try them out in training first. I like PowerBars or Cytobars, both specially prepared energy foods designed with the needs of endurance athletes in mind. Rice cakes are easy to digest, but very low in calories. Rice pudding can be easily carried in a spare drinks bottle. Bananas and dried fruit work well for some people but might have an alarming effect on your bowels. Jam sandwiches (without butter or margarine) are good, too.

You must also eat as soon as possible after a race, to help your body to replenish its depleted glycogen stores. As usual, you should opt for high carbohydrate, low-fat foods, although you can indulge in slightly more fat after a race. Eating simple carbohydrates in the first six hours after a race helps your body to restore its muscle glycogen more readily. The more exhaustive your activity, the more urgent the need to replenish carbohydrate as soon as possible after you stop. In addition, eccentric exercise – such as running downhill – which produces muscle damage and soreness also requires a larger helping hand in the glycogen replenishing stakes.

Drinking

It is of paramount importance to keep well hydrated both in day to day life and during races. You will lose two to three litres of sweat per hour during a triathlon. The volume of sweat lost increases in heat and humidity and is greater for heat acclimatised and better trained people.

If you do not replace the fluids lost during exertion, you would soon find yourself in a state of dehydration. This impairs exercise capacity, reduces your blood volume and cardiac output and can even be life-threatening.

Fluids are as important to your muscles as an adequate intake of carbohydrate. Along with glycogen, your muscles store water. A well hydrated muscle is more flexible, and is able to stretch and contract effectively. When the muscle becomes dehydrated, it becomes more brittle, is more prone to damage and needs longer to recover from training sessions.

During a race, you should start drinking before you feel thirsty. Have a drink bottle handy at the transition area and drink just after getting out of the water. Then, have another sip of your drink 15 minutes into the bike ride, and continue to drink every 15 minutes or so. Ideally, combine your fluid and energy needs by drinking a sports drink, as outlined above. On the bike, drinking in the region of 1000 ml or one large waterbottle per hour will help to maintain bodyweight and

There is more than one way to empty a water bottle during a triathlon. You can either drink the contents or pour them over your head to keep cool. Before you choose the latter check the contents – some sports drinks are very sticky

plasma volume and will enhance endurance. During the run, 100 to 200 ml every two to three kilometres will serve the same purpose. As little as a two percent loss in bodyweight during a race will have a negative effect on performance.

Also remember to have a drink at the poolside during training sessions. Many triathletes neglect hydration when they are in the water – one of the sport's many ironies.

A great many variables can affect your fluid absorption, including the caloric density of the drink, the temperature of the drink, the air temperature, humidity, time of day, even, if you are female, the phase of your menstrual cycle. Listen to the signals your body is sending you. If you drink a lot of coffee, tea or alcohol, your need to replenish fluids will be increased, as all are diuretics.

Sarah Springman's eating tips

As a triathlete, there are certain periods in your athletic progression when you are prepared to make sacrifices, particularly in your diet, in order to be the best. In 1987, a lot of top British triathletes were adopting the Pritikin style of eating (very low fat and high carbohydrate) and reading books like Robert Haas' Eat to Win. A day's eating included lots of pasta, maybe some tomato sauce, tuna for protein (water-packed, of course), lots of salad with no dressing, and vast quantities of fruit and no caffeinated beverages. These days, some cottage cheese or Parmesan might garnish the pasta, but otherwise, the blueprint remains the same.

Try to follow these rules:

1 *Make sure you get plenty of natural minerals and vitamins, which you can get from fresh fruit and vegetables, and by following a balanced diet.*

2 *Take a supplement. You must make certain that you aren't lacking in essential minerals and vitamins. If you are, you won't be able to convert all the energy you need, you will feel tired, you won't be able to get the most out of yourself. Try taking about 50% of the daily vitamin and mineral dose recommended by the manufacturer of your brand of vitamins. A healthy and balanced diet should provide a large proportion of the vitamins and minerals that you need.*

3 *Drink a lot of fluids. If you are partial to caffeinated drinks, drink even more water. You should be urinating frequently, and your urine should be clear in colour. If it is dark and concentrated, you are verging on dehydration.*

4 *If you want to lose weight, determine the amount of energy you expend in training plus the amount required to maintain basic body functions, and match your calorie intake to it. You will need to take in fewer calories than you are burning, but remember that you will still need some energy, or calories, as fuel. Crash diets (less than 1500 calories a day) are out of the question.*

5 *Again, if you want to lose weight, try to concentrate your caloric intake earlier in the day. This gives your body less chance to store excess calories as fat. So, have a big breakfast, a medium-size lunch and a small dinner.*

APPROXIMATE GUIDE TO KILOCALORIC EXPENDITURE PER MINUTE

Weight:	100 lbs	120 lbs	140 lbs	150 lbs	160 lbs	180 lbs	200 lbs
Cycling							
10 mph	5	7	8	8	9	10	11
15 mph	8	9	10	11	12	13	14
20 mph	13	14	16	16½	17	183	19
25 mph	18	19	20	20½	26	27	28
30 mph	23	24	25	25½	26	27	28
Running							
10 mpm	7	8	10	11	12	14	16
8 mpm	911	14	15	16	18	19	
6 mpm	12	14	18	19	20	21	22
5 mpm	13	16	20	21	22	24	26
Swimming (crawl)							
30 mpm	6	7	9	9½	10	11	12
26 mpm	9½	10½	12	12½	13	15	16
22mpm	13	14	12	15½	16	19	20
17 mpm	16	17	19	19½	20	21	24

mph = miles per hour   mpm = minutes per mile

6 *Remember: you can lose too much weight. If you do, your immune system will not be at par, and you will probably lose strength on the bike. We tend to each have optimal weights, which are individually determined*

and will not be found in any tables or books. As a triathlete, you need to try to find the balance between a weight that will allow you to run to the best of your ability, to not lose strength on the bike, and to maintain a healthy immune defence mechanism, which will allow you to train regularly, without interruptions from recurring bugs.

Calorie management

Six-time Ironman winner Dave Scott reckons he can store around 3500 calories worth of glycogen if he carbo-loads, but an Ironman distance race is going to cost someone of Scott's height and weight in the region of 8,000 to 10,000 calories.

Obviously, there is going to be a deficit. Eating 5,000 to 7,000 calories worth of food in the time it takes to complete the Ironman is physically impossible unless you were to set up a banquet table at the roadside and, literally, stuff your face. (This is undesirable, as it would cost you a lot of time . . .) But people do get through Ironman triathlons without breaking down. They burn fat.

To metabolise fat, you have to be working at between 70–85% of your maximum pace. This usually corresponds to 70–85% of your maximum heart rate range, where 85% is anaerobic threshold, and 70% is your aerobic threshold. The closer you are to your aerobic threshold, the more fat you're burning. And the more you train yourself at your aerobic threshold, the more efficient your body becomes

Day	Diet CHO Meat Milk Fruit Veg Fat Total	Physical	Psychological
Monday			
Tuesday			
Wednesday			
Thursday			
Friday			
Saturday			
Sunday			
Swim km	0 1 2 3 4 5 6 7 8 9 10 11 12 14 15 16 17 18 19 20		Stretch mins
Bike miles	0 50 100 150 200 250 300 350 400		Wts mins
Run miles	0 5 10 15 20 25 30 35 40 45 50 55 60		Mental Rehearsal mins

Keep a record of food intake, energy expenditure and how you feel, mentally and physically. You can refer back to your diary to find the best diet and training formula for you

at burning fat. This is the reason for those long, slow distance runs in a build-up to an Ironman.

Assume for now that at 75% of your maximum pace you burn 50% fat and 50% carbohydrate. If you did the whole race like that, you would be looking at an equal number of calories coming out of fat and out of whatever food you are taking in.

In a long race such as the Ironman, you can take in about two grammes of carbohydrate per kilo of bodyweight per hour. So, a 70kg triathlete competing in a long, lesser intensity race – in which the body can cope with slightly higher percentages of sugar than it would be able to in a shorter, more intense race – should be able to assimilate 140 grammes of carbohydrate per hour, along with sufficient water. If one gramme of carbohydrate equals four calories, then that carbohydrate intake is equivalent to around 560 calories, or two PowerBars and one banana.

The most effective way to take in this energy is in sports energy drinks. These are carbohydrate drinks, not electrolyte, or isotonic, drinks. If your diet and fluid intake are balanced leading up to the race, you are unlikely to have an electrolyte deficit during or after the race. Cytomax and Maxim come highly recommended. You should be sipping at this energy drink at all times throughout the race, and you will probably also need to eat some solid foods during an Ironman: bananas, energy bars . . . test your menu before the race.

For a half-Ironman, try 1 to 1 ½ grammes of carbohydrate per kilo of bodyweight per hour. For a 50kg woman, that would mean 50 grammes of carbohydrate per hour, or approximately 200 calories. Your need for solid foods to provide the calories will not be as great as during an Ironman.

There is no magical diet that will make you into a super-athlete. You need to experiment and find what is right for you.

Springman's tip: *I tend to put a concentrated solution of my chosen drink, which I've tested thoroughly in training, in a Bikestream, and then carry two diluted bottles of the same drink on the bike. When I've finished the bottles, I replace their content with pure water and sip at the concentrated solution, washing it down with water.*

Grab a sponge as you run through the feed station: sponging yourself down will help you to stay cool

CHAPTER 4

The principles of training

Why do you train? The answer, without looking for psychological reasons, is simple: you train to condition your body. During training, you place stress on your body, and your body adapts to cope with it. So, if you do lots of long slow distance training, you will become very efficient at running, swimming or cycling over long distances at slow speed. You will not, however, have the sprint needed to burn off the competition in the finishing straight. The changes your body undergoes during training are specific to the type of training you do.

The type of training you concentrate on should vary according to your short- and long-term goals. If, for instance, you have just started in triathlon and your immediate goal is an event with an 800 metre swim, 30km bike ride and 5km run, your needs will, obviously, be very different to those of the more experienced triathlete who is aiming to peak for the Hawaii Ironman.

However, you can expect to see similarities between the programmes of the sprint distance triathlete and the Ironman hopeful. Both should follow mixed programmes of training, ie regimes which train the energy systems used to sprint, to race hard over medium distances and to keep going for races of several hours' duration. Each activity places the body under different types of stress and has different physiological benefits for the athlete.

In any physical activity, your muscles contract and relax. In order to do so, the muscles need fuel, and they get this fuel in the form of adenosine triphosphate, or ATP. ATP is formed by breaking down carbohydrate, which is present in the body either because you have taken on carbohydrate – ie eaten or drunk carbohydrate-rich foods – during or just before a race, or in the form of glycogen. Glycogen is, quite simply, stored carbohydrate. It is found in the muscles and liver and can provide enough energy for roughly two hours of activity.

Your muscles can contract aerobically, or with oxygen which they use to oxidise the ATP, or without oxygen (anaerobically). The energy a muscle can release in the absence of oxygen is very limited, compared to the amount it can produce aerobically.

A good analogy is used by Per-Olof Astrand in his *Textbook of Work Physiology*. He compares car engines to the human engine. Both need fuel to work: the car petrol, the body ATP. Petrol is oxidised, or burnt, as you cruise along the motorway for hours on end. Similarly, when you go out on a long, slow training run, you use oxygen to produce energy. Both the car and the human body stop working when their fuel tanks are empty.

Alternatively, you can turn over the car engine by stepping on the starter and letting the battery do all the work – the body's equivalent to exercising anaerobically. Without oxygen, the car engine can only turn over for a short time. Similarly, the energy a muscle can release in the absence of oxygen is limited, compared to the energy it can produce aerobically.

There are three systems by which your body produces energy:

ATP-CP (*Adenosine triphosphate-creatine phosphate*) ATP kicks into action at the onset of exercise. During the energy production process, it loses one phosphate molecule and becomes adenosine diphosphate (ADP). Another substance also stored in the muscles, creatine phosphate (CP) combines with ADP to resynthesize ATP. This process occurs anaerobically (without oxygen) and can, in theory, continue until you run out of creatine phosphate – or for approximately 30 seconds. It is believed that the level of CP stored in muscles can be increased by sprint training.

When you run out of CP, you need to find another means of resynthesizing ATP, so your body switches to another energy system:

ATP-Lactic Acid As you deplete the CP in your muscles, glycogen begins to break down through a process called anaerobic glycolysis. This process produces a by-product called pyruvic acid, which provides high energy phosphates which can change ADP into ATP. Pyruvic acid then picks up a hydrogen ion and forms lactic acid, a substance often singled out as the main culprit causing muscle stiffness.

In fact, lactic acid isn't all bad. You need it to sustain short, high intensity efforts lasting between 30 seconds and two minutes. You run into problems when you produce lactic acid in excess, can't diffuse it properly to the working muscles or can't use it to resynthesize glycogen. All these factors depend on your physical make-up and also on the level of exertion you are trying to maintain while exercising. If you are pushing yourself as hard or as fast as possible, then your body will be less able to diffuse or resynthesize lactic acid than if you were exercising aerobically.

Using the ATP-Lactic Acid system of energy, you will eventually build up an oxygen debt and lactic acid concentration. The point at which you can just still clear lactic acid from your muscles is called your *anaerobic threshold*.

The anaerobic threshold varies from person to person. It is, in practical terms, the point of maximum power and highest speed which you can maintain for a reasonably long period of time without slowing – around 30 minutes. Anaerobic threshold can be determined in the laboratory by testing blood lactate levels. When blood lactate is elevated – above one to two mmol per litre of blood – and also accumulating in the blood, ie not being diffused back into the system, you have reached your anaerobic threshold. The difference between you and Spencer Smith might be that your blood lactate tests will reveal four mmols/l at a lower level of effort than the 1993 world champion's.

Lactate clearance, or the ability to work at your anaerobic threshold, has often been used as a measure of fitness. To clear lactic acid from your muscle tissue, it has to bond with oxygen and be carried into the bloodstream. There, it will be neutralised, resynthesized or excreted in the urine.

Physical training enhances the rate of lactate clearance by improving your oxidative capacity. It has been shown, too, that ingesting lactate orally can improve lactate clearance capacity; some manufacturers of sports drinks

have recognised this fact and include a percentage of lactate in their sports drinks.

After the ATP-CP and ATP-lactic acid phases, which are characterised by breathlessness and the discomfort experienced at the start of a training session, the body starts to derive ATP aerobically. Enough oxygen is available to the muscles to oxidise and resynthesize lactic acid into glycogen. Working aerobically, you can continue almost indefinitely, the limiting factor being the availability of oxygen to the muscle cells. There is no lactic acid accumulation, no oxygen debt. You are now in:

Steady state training During long training sessions or triathlons, glycogen and fat are used as the main sources of energy, the latter being broken down into glycerol and free fatty acids and then being released into the bloodstream. The ratio of glycogen to fat used to produce energy during long efforts varies from person to person and also depends on factors such as your starting speed, the amount of glycogen stored in your muscles and your recent food and drink intake.

The fitter you are, the more efficient your body will be at burning fat. As the body can store about 50,000 Calories of energy in the form of fat in the tissues and bloodstream, the endurance potential for efficient fat-burning bodies is almost endless.

An exercise programme which uses each of these energy systems will tax

Eureka! You've done it! Whether it's the Ironman or a local race reaching the finish in a triathlon is always a cause for celebration

Sometimes the effort is
all too much. France's
Yves Cordier finished
third in the 1991 Nice
Triathlon, but was
totally spent at the end
of the race

your muscles totally, thus stimulating the kind of all-round muscle development a triathlete needs. In other words, as a result of training, the functional constituents of a muscle – the parts called into play by a given activity – will adapt specifically according to whether the exercise you do stresses the endurance (aerobic) or strength/speed (anaerobic) energy systems.

How efficient you become at sprinting versus long, slow distance work depends in part on your genetic make-up. If you find that you are better at tackling endurance work, it means that you have inherited a predominance of slow-twitch muscle fibres from your parents. If you are more adept at sprint/strength work, you have a predominance of fast-twitch muscle fibres. No muscle can accommodate maximal aerobic and anaerobic adaptations, ie you cannot create a muscle that is as good at sprinting as it is at distance work. Through training, however, you can change the composition of a muscle.

Most of the work you do in a triathlon will be steady state work, but at the beginning of a race you will call on your ATP-CP system and your ATP-lactic acid system will be activated several times during the race. To train all three energy systems, your programme should include:

Sprint training
85% anaerobic and 15% aerobic activity, sprint training requires an all-out effort over a short distance (15 to 30 seconds), with a 20 to 30 second rest interval. (In running, the rest interval should be roughly twice as long as the effort.) Sprint training increases strength and the muscles' ability to contract quickly, ie your ability to sprint. It is also believed that sprint training, over a period of time, improves the ability to sustain an all-out effort.
Perceived effort: very hard. Percentage of effort to theoretical heart-rate maximum: 90 to 100%.

VO$_2$ Max training
50–70% anaerobic and 30–50% aerobic activity, VO$_2$ Max training consists of hard efforts that are longer than those in sprint training (three to eight minutes) with long rest intervals. Use the following rest guidelines during VO$_2$ Max training:

Swimming: four work intervals, one rest interval
Cycling: two work intervals, one rest interval
Running: one work interval, one rest interval

For example, if during a VO$_2$ Max session you were to run for three minutes, you should rest for the same amount of time. On the other hand, if you swim for four minutes at VO$_2$ Max level, you should rest for one minute.
Perceived effort: hard. Percentage of effort to theoretical heart-rate maximum: 80 to 95%.

During VO$_2$ Max sessions, energy is

supplied mainly through the anaerobic breakdown of glycogen in the muscles. There is a high level of oxygen debt, but it is repaid during the rest periods. The heart stroke volume is high, and remains high during the rest intervals, pumping more blood and, therefore, more oxygen to the working muscles. Your VO_2 Max, ie the maximum volume of oxygen your body can absorb during exercise, is improved by this kind of exercise, which increases the number of capillaries and the number and quality of mitochondria – tiny cellules in the muscle fibres, part of whose job it is to release the ATP used during aerobic work – in the muscle cells. VO_2 Max is expressed in terms of millilitres of oxygen consumed per minute per kilogram of body weight. Therefore, the quickest way to improve your VO_2 Max is to lose a couple of pounds.

Anaerobic Threshold Training

15–45% anaerobic and 55–85% aerobic activity, anaerobic threshold training consists of moderate effort with short rest intervals, or a constant effort over 20 to 30 minutes. You are working at your anaerobic threshold when you are at a point of exertion which just allows lactic acid to begin to diffuse back into your bloodstream, where it can be used as fuel. In everyday terms, anaerobic threshold training has been described as the point at which a seven-word sentence just requires a breath to complete. Anaerobic threshold training is thought by many top triathletes to be the key to

triathlon success.

During the short rest intervals that are part of anaerobic threshold training, ATP and CP can be replenished to some extent, thus delaying the accumulation of lactic acid. This means that you can work harder than you would during a long, slow distance session. Anaerobic threshold training also teaches your body to burn a greater proportion of fatty acids to glycogen, and therefore makes you more fuel efficient.

If you only reach your anaerobic threshold at 90% of your maximum effort level, you will be able to run, swim and cycle faster than the triathletes who hit theirs at 75% of their maximum.

Perceived effort: moderate to hard. Percentage of effort to theoretical heart-rate maximum: 75 to 90%.

Distance training

5–30% anaerobic and 70–95% aerobic activity, distance training is characterised by a sustained continuous effort. It stresses the oxygen transport system in your body, resulting in:

● increased cardiac output and an improved heart capacity to pump more blood with each beat (stroke volume)
● a lower resting pulse rate, which is indicative of improved stroke volume
● better oxygenation of the blood
● improved lung capacity
● enhanced glycogen storage in the liver and muscles

- increased number of capillaries and mitochondria in the muscles
- improved ability to burn fat as fuel, thus sparing glycogen stores.

Distance training, lasting anywhere from 15 minutes to several hours, will improve your endurance capacity both psychologically and physiologically. *Perceived effort*: easy/moderate. Percentage of effort to theoretical heart-rate maximum: 60 to 80%.

Determining effort levels

It is difficult, if not impossible, to determine your VO_2 Max or anaerobic threshold without undergoing tests in a laboratory. A lot of athletes depend on perceived exertion and/or a pulse monitor to determine if they are training at the desired level.

Anaerobic efforts are characterised by breathlessness, muscle discomfort and a greatly elevated heart rate – 80% and upwards of your theoretical maximum. This kind of effort can only be sustained for a short period of time.

When you train aerobically, on the other hand, your pulse rate should be at approximately 60 to 70% of your theoretical maximum. Breathing will be heavy, but you should be able to conduct a conversation when exercising aerobically.

Determining your pulse rate
When you first start training, learn to understand what your pulse rate is trying to tell you. To do this,

determine your resting pulse rate by taking your pulse for one minute first thing in the morning over several days, and averaging out the findings. Then, determine your maximum heart rate. This can be found most simply by subtracting your age from 220 if you are a man, 226 for a woman. Next, subtract your resting pulse rate from your maximum heart rate, which will give you a figure known as your range.

To determine what your pulse rate should be when you are exercising at 60% of your theoretical maximum, ie the bottom of your aerobic workout level, multiply your range figure by .6 and then add your resting pulse rate. So, if you are a 30-year old male and your resting pulse rate is 40, an aerobic workout pulse rate would be determined like this:

Resting pulse rate: 40 bpm
Maximum pulse rate: $220 - 30 = 190$
Range: $190 - 40 = 150$
60% of maximum: $(.6 \times 150) + 40 = 90 + 40 = 130$

Remember: your pulse rate can be anywhere between 60 and 80% of your theoretical maximum when you are working aerobically. 70% of your maximum would be determined thus: $(.7 \times 150) + 40 = 155$. To arrive at the figure for 80%, multiply your range by .8 and add your resting pulse.

Your anaerobic threshold should, in theory, be occurring at around 85% of your maximum. Therefore, for a 30-year old male, $(.85 \times 150) + 40 = $ approx 167 bpm.

Regular sprint and
interval training will
help you when you
need that burst of speed
to burn off the
competition in the
finishing straight

The best way to monitor your pulse rate is by wearing a pulse monitor. If one is out of your budget, then you can monitor your pulse rate by taking a reading immediately after exertion. Count your pulse over six seconds and then tag a zero onto the end of the total figure. For example, if you have just sprinted hard for 100 metres, stop afterwards and take your pulse over six seconds. If it is 19, then adding a zero onto the end of that figure will leave you with a pulse rate of 190 beats per minute.

If you are unable to train with a pulse monitor, learn to equate what training at 190 beats per minute feels like with physical sensations — what is called 'perceived effort'. That way, you won't have to stop after every sprint session to take your pulse. Were you breathless while sprinting? Did you begin to feel a hint of stiffness in your muscles? Was the effort sustainable for just a short period of time? When you do anaerobic threshold sessions, are you able to utter, say, a seven-word sentence? How do your muscles feel? How fast is your breathing? Make a mental note of the sensations for each type of training, so that you know what to work towards in your next session.

If you should wake up one morning and find your pulse is elevated by more than 10 beats a minute above its usual rate, consider taking a day off. You are either coming down with something, or you are overtraining, or both. (See also Chapter 12 Injuries).

There is one method for determining your anaerobic threshold that is non-invasive, ie doesn't require anyone to stick needles into you. That's the Conconi test, named after the Italian doctor who invented it. To conduct it, you need a pulse monitor, a willing friend on a bike with a cyclo-computer to measure speed, and a running track.

Run 200 metres at a given speed, and in the last 50 metres of the 200, check your pulse monitor and shout out your pulse rate to your pacer on the bike in front of you. For the next 200, your pacer should increase his or her speed by 1/2 mph, and you should increase your running speed accordingly. Continue increasing the speed at which you are running by 1/2 mph for each 200, always noting your pulse rate in the last 50 metres of each 200, and shouting it out to your pacer, who will jot it down. When fatigue stops you from increasing your pace for another 200 metres, warm down and end the session.

Next, plot your pulse-rate levels during the Conconi test session on a graph. The result should be a sloping curve, with the point where you couldn't go any faster marked by a kink in the graph. This is your anaerobic threshold.

The test can also be performed on a bike (300 – 450 metres per lap, increasing speeds by one mph), or you can use a treadmill or turbo-trainer instead of a track, increasing the speed after a set time interval, eg one minute, rather than distance. By retesting yourself periodically, you can monitor your training progress. You should find that your anaerobic threshold improves, ie the kink occurs later in the graph, as you get fitter.

The Conconi test works from some, and is inconclusive for others. The advantage is that it is non-invasive and doesn't need lab conditions to try it. If it proves successful for you the results will at least give you a starting point for your anaerobic training sessions.

Genetic influence

You will find that one sort of training comes more easily to you than another. This depends largely on your body composition – your percentage of body fat and the type of muscle fibres that predominate in your make-up.

Body fat usually reduces as you take up training, assuming that you follow a sound, low-fat and high-carbohydrate diet that is not excessive in calories. Top female triathletes tend to have around 13% to 15% body fat, while their male counterparts boast just seven to eight percent. A moderately trained triathlete who follows a sensible diet can easily achieve 18% to 22% (women) and 13% to 15% (men).

More difficult to change is muscle composition. All of us are born with both fast- and slow-twitch muscle fibres, but in different proportions.

On the final straight of any triathlon you'll reap the benefits of intelligent training

Most muscles are a mix of these two types of fibre. If you are endowed with an abundance of slow-twitch muscle, whose fibres have large numbers of mitochondria, are rich in myoglobin, a protein substance related to haemoglobin, and which can contract and release repeatedly for long periods without fatigue, then you are more likely to be a better marathon runner than sprinter. If, on the other hand, you have a large number of fast-twitch cells – fewer mitochondria and less haemoglobin – then your muscles will use up their oxygen supply much more quickly than slow-twitch muscle fibres, but they can contract three times faster, which means you are endowed with more sprinting and strength talent than endurance.

There are oxidative and anaerobic fast-twitch fibres, and it is possible to train the oxidative ones to act more like slow-twitch fibres by increasing their number of mitochondria through distance training. You cannot change a fast-twitch into a slow-twitch muscle; you can simply alter the balance of the muscle's composition.

Understanding your body composition is an important preliminary step in planning a training programme. Naturally, you need to work on improving your weaknesses, but by the same token, you must accept your limitations. If you were born with a preponderance of slow-twitch fibres, which predisposes you to distance work, accept the fact and make the most of it.

The training year

We all have days when we feel as if we have been working flat-out from the minute we get out of bed until the moment we fall back into it. Fortunately, even the most hectic of days is made up of intermittent activity: you stop for lunch or to take a phone call. In between these moments of relative calm, you might be running at full pelt, but it is impossible to function at 110% continuously.

Training works in the same way, both on a day-to-day basis and in the training year. You need to divide your training into phases:

1 Rest and build
This phase is divided into three sub-phases. During the first, which falls immediately after the close of your triathlon season, allow yourself a break. Run, swim or cycle for pleasure, at greatly reduced intensity. Play squash, ski, mountain climb, hike in the woods. Don't opt for the television and Mars Bar rest and recuperation method: it will only help the unwanted pounds to sneak onto your frame and will make restarting triathlon training that much harder.

2 Rest and build phases 2 and 3
Aim to build a sturdy foundation for the rest of your triathlon year. Concentrate on building strength and endurance. This requires the training of your fast- and slow-twitch muscle fibres, something achieved by calling different energy systems into play.

Concentrate on aerobic training in phase two of the rest and build phase, adding strength and anaerobic threshold workouts in phase three. Training intensity and duration should increase gradually over the two periods.

Remember that in any of the phases, you should never increase intensity, duration or the number of work-outs drastically. The 10 percent rule is a good one to follow: only increase intensity or duration by 10 percent when an increase is warranted, ie when a session becomes easy and you are recovering quickly and fully afterwards.

3 Pre-season

During this phase, you will be spending a great deal of time doing anaerobic threshold work, which is arguably the backbone of triathlon success. Strength training will be cut back, but technique work should be maintained if there is a need. Concentrate on your weaknesses during this phase. If you falter on short, steep hills, concentrate on sprint workouts. If long, steady climbs wear you out before the halfway mark, increase VO_2 Max and distance training. Add sprint training to all three sports. Some triathletes, Springman included, maintain some sprint training all year round, because it helps them to maintain good form.

4 Pre-competition

Begin to hone your training to fit in with your racing. This phase begins about six weeks before your first event, with a time trial or Conconi test to assess improvements in all three sports since the beginning of your training schedule. Depending on the length and type of event you will be doing in six weeks' time, and on the results of your time trial/Conconi test, tailor your training to ensure that you are in top form when the event arrives. If, for instance, a 10km running time trial shows a drop in performance since you started training, you could be overtraining. During the pre-competition phase, you should tweak your training schedule to compensate: allow more rest time and cut back on very stressful sessions. Slower times could also mean that you have concentrated too much on long, slow distance work, and have become efficient at running long distances, but very slowly. Check your training diary and make any changes necessary to ensure that on race day you have the speed and endurance you need to perform at your best.

Generally, during the pre-competition phase, you will be reducing distance and VO_2 Max sessions, but will increase sprint and anaerobic threshold training. Times realised over a given distance during anaerobic threshold sessions should be at or near your target race times during this phase. If they are way off the mark, your should reassess your goals.

5 Competition

In the week or fortnight before a race, your physical training and mental preparation should be focused on the forthcoming event. Ease up on your training, especially on very taxing sessions. Have a very easy day two days before the race.

This is sometimes referred to as a taper period, and the intention is to leave you as fresh and strong as possible for the event you plan to do. Gear your diet toward the race, ie concentrate on eating plenty of carbohydrate so that your glycogen stores are replete. Remember, however, that when you eat a lot of carbohydrate, you also store water. Find the right balance, so that you go into the race with rich stores of glycogen, without feeling heavy.

Everyone has a different level to which they can cut back their training without losing form. Find yours by experimenting before races that aren't as important to you as, say, the world championships qualifiers. It's useful to seek the advice of a coach on this matter.

Increase your stretching routine to do more in the week or fortnight before a race; avoid alcohol for at least the two days immediately preceding a big event, and preferably for a week beforehand. Some athletes like to have a massage two days before a race.

Immediately after the race, allow your body a day or two to recover. The best way to do this is through what's called active rest sessions, these are training sessions at 60 to 70% effort. Then, return to high-quality sessions, the backbone of a competition season's training schedule.

One very important thing to remember during the racing season is that your body needs time to recover. You need to find the right balance of recovery and training/racing time so that you can take your peak fitness into races with you, not leave it on the training circuit.

If the above periods lasted one month each, then three rest and build phases, one pre-season, pre-competition and competition phase could take you through six months. You can alter the schedule – by shortening the duration of each phase, for instance – and peak for a big race at any time of year. But remember that your body can only cope with a given amount of stress, and if you try to peak for a race every month or weekend, you will probably only disappoint yourself. You can't expect your body to perform to its maximum that often.

Six weeks is a useful time frame to allot to training phases, or even to a miniature training 'year'. It allows your body and motor functions time to adapt to the stresses to which you are submitting them. If you are just beginning in triathlon, you might want to limit your racing to one event every six weeks, allowing yourself mini-phases – rest and build, hone and race – in between events. Your six-week schedule might look something like the following:

Week 1 Race Sunday. Easy week of active rest sessions afterwards.

Week 2 Build. Concentrate on VO_2 Max and anaerobic threshold sessions, but maintain all four kinds of training.

Week 3 Build. As in Week 2, but increase intensity of training if your recovery times and progress allow. Start to increase sprint training. Distances should be near or at their peak.

Week 4 Hone. More sprint and anaerobic threshold training, reaching a peak for both around mid-week. Begin to cut back on VO_2 Max training. Maintain distance training.

Week 5 Hone. If you are having trouble recovering, begin to cut sprint sessions in the middle of the week, but try not to exclude them entirely. If need be, allow longer rest periods, during and between sessions, to allow for high quality work. Anaerobic threshold and VO_2 Max sessions should be incorporated in distance training.

Week 6 Peak. Cut back on stressful sprint, VO_2 Max and anaerobic threshold sessions. Precisely when you cut back — usually two to four days before a race — will depend on you and your body's preferences. Have a very easy day two days or so before a race; again, this will depend on your own preferences.

Putting theory into practice

By mixing and matching all the elements of training in the right ratio for the time of year, you should arrive at a balanced programme. Those ratios should look something like this:

Build and pre-season phases
Swim Sprint: 1/2
VO_2 Max 2/4
Anaerobic threshold: 3
Distance: 3/4

Bike Sprint: 1
VO_2 Max: 1/2
Anaerobic threshold: 4
Distance: 4

Run Sprint: 1
VO_2 Max 1
Anaerobic threshold: 2/3
Distance 3/4

Competitive
Swim Sprint: 3
VO_2 Max: 3
Anaerobic threshold: 5
Distance: 4

Bike Sprint: 3
VO_2 Max: 2
Anaerobic threshold: 3
Distance: 4

Run Sprint: 2
VO_2 Max: 2
Anaerobic threshold: 3
Distance: 3

Remember: these are ratios. If you do one sprint session in the pool during the pre-season phase, for instance, you should be doing one to two distance sessions. In addition, both types of training can be incorporated into one session – in other words, you don't need to swim 11 times a week during the pre-season!

Build up to these ratios slowly and gradually, but try to stay true to them. What you should notice is that the emphasis during the early phases of training is on anaerobic threshold and distance work. Sprints and VO_2 Max workouts become more important as the season wears on, for honing and maintaining form.

Post-competitive

Sprint and VO_2 Max sessions fade away. Concentrate on occasional anaerobic threshold sessions for variety, but mainly on moderate, steady distance work.

The possibilities for creating interesting and varied sessions that contain a good mix of all the training elements are numerous. Some are listed below.

Swimming

Warm up, 400 metres any or all strokes, easy.
Technique drills
One arm Swim using one arm only. Change arms every 25 or 50 metres. Do 4 x 50 metres (4 x 100 if you are more advanced) with ten seconds' rest in between each 50 (one rep). More advanced swimmers can do two sets of 4 x 50 or 4 x 100, resting 30 seconds to one minute between sets.

Catch-up Swim with arms extended in front of you. Do the freestyle stroke with the right arm. At the end of the stroke, allow both hands to meet in front of you and extend forward from the shoulders. Then, repeat with the left arm. Continue alternating arms, hands pausing in front and reaching forward. Concentrate on getting hold of, or 'catching' the water (see Chapter 5) and on elongating your stroke by extending forward from the shoulders. Do reps and sets as for one arm.

High elbow While swimming freestyle concentrate on keeping your elbows high during the recovery section. To facilitate this, touch the fingertips of the working arm to your shoulder before your hand re-enters the water. Reps and sets as above.

Arms-only Swim using a pullbuoy. Concentrate on all aspects of the freestyle stroke. Reps and sets as above.

For a new triathlete, especially one who is not from a swimming background, the above warm-up, plus one set each of the technique drills and a 200 metre warm down will add up to 1200 metres and will complete one session.

Below are examples of sprint, VO_2 Max and anaerobic threshold training, which can be incorporated into your training sessions.

Sprint training
8 x 50 metres at 100–120% effort. Rest 15 to 20 seconds between each rep.

VO₂ Max training

8 x 100, hard effort with a 20-second rest between reps. As you get fitter, reduce the rest time.

Or try: 4 x 100 with a 20-second rest between reps; 2 x 200 metres with a 10-second rest. One minute between sets, then repeat.

Or 4 x 100 metres kicking, with a 15-second rest between reps. More advance swimmers can do two sets with a 30-second rest between sets.

Anaerobic threshold training

The same distances and sets as used in VO₂ Max training can be altered slightly to produce anaerobic threshold training sessions. Effort should be decreased slightly, and the rest intervals should be shorter.

Try: 3 x 200 metres with a 20-second rest between each repetition. Take a 30-second rest between sets and then go into 6 x 100 metres with 15 seconds between reps. Maintain your times for each 100. During the rest intervals, your pulse rate should drop. The longer the rest interval, the more significant the drop in pulse rate should be.

Distance training

2 x 800 metres, 30 seconds between each. Maintain times.

Or: 800 metres, out slow, back fast. Swim the first 200 metres at a pace slower than the next 200 metres, which should be swum at or near race pace.

Then slow down again, only to pick up the pace for the last 200 metres. Rest 45 seconds and repeat. This session is helpful in teaching you to accelerate in the second half of an effort, and by varying your speeds, you also break up the monotony of a long swim.

All-round training Swim as fast as you can for 100 metres and note your time. Add one minute to that time. The total will give you your interval time for the first of 10 x 100 metres to follow.

So, if you swim your first 100 metres in 1:30, your first 100 in the set will be swum off 2:30, ie you don't set off for the next 100 until 2:30 minutes have elapsed on the clock. That means the faster you swim your 100, the more time you'll have to rest. The second 100 will be swum off 2:20, the third off 2:10, with interval times descending by 10 seconds per repetition until you are left with your 100 time plus no more than 10 seconds rest (you should have swum 6 x 100 metres). Swim another 4 x 100 metres: in this example, they would be swum off 1:40. If you have slowed down over the session, you will have less than 10 seconds' rest in the final 4 x 100. If you've maintained your time, you will have 10 seconds between 100s. This session takes you through 1000 metres (distance) and trains your VO₂ Max and anaerobic threshold systems.

Cycling

Sprint: ride hard up hills or on the flat. Maintain the sprint effort for 20 seconds to one minute. Rest, by pedalling easily, until your heart rate returns to your aerobic level, and repeat. Incorporating sprint sessions into a distance session on the bike will pep up your training without causing over-tiredness.

A good way to train your sprint system on the bike is on a turbo-trainer. Set up your bike on the turbo-trainer. Warm up by spinning gently for 10 minutes, gradually increasing the intensity. Then do:

4 x 1 minute hard effort with 45 seconds rest between each. After the set, spin for 10 minutes in an easy gear; then repeat the sprint session. Warm down 10 minutes, spinning an easy gear.

Note: you should have a very good mileage base in your legs before beginning VO_2 Max or sprint training – at least 1000 cycling miles! In general, most triathletes should concentrate on training levels up to and including anaerobic threshold on the bike, bringing in some VO_2 Max sessions as the competition season approaches. Sprint training should be introduced to hone your training in the six weeks prior to a target race.

VO₂ Max and anaerobic threshold
The above sprint session can be translated into VO_2 Max and anaerobic threshold sessions by lengthening the time of the efforts and decreasing their intensity. VO_2 Max rest intervals should be longer than those in anaerobic threshold training, as the intensity of effort is higher. In between sets, spin for five minutes on a VO_2 Max session, one to two minutes for an anaerobic threshold session.

A VO_2 Max turbo-trainer session might look something like this: two minutes perceived hard effort, with 45 seconds to one minute recovery, repeated four to five times. Then spin easily for five minutes and repeat.

Anaerobic threshold: two minutes at moderate to hard perceived intensity, with 30 to 45 seconds' rest: four to five times. Two minutes' easy spinning, then repeat twice more.

Distance training
Turbo-trainers are not recommended for distance sessions. The boredom factor is too great! The best way to get your distance workouts on the bike is to go out with a group of cyclists on their Sunday ride.

Running
Sprint training
The best place to do sprint training for running is on a track. As usual, warm up first, then try: 4 x 100 metres at 100–120% effort (very hard perceived effort). Jog the remainder of the track and repeat. After 4 x 100 metres, jog 400 metres at a steady but relaxed pace. Then, repeat the set. Warm down at the end.

VO₂ Max/Anaerobic threshold
After a steady run to warm up, run

Stair climbing is said to
be one of the most
effective cardio-
vascular exercises. If
you can do it in the
open air, all the better

4 x 800 metres at 80–90% effort (hard) with 1:30 easy jogging in between. Aim to match or better your current 10kms race time. Or do:

4 x 400 metres with descending rest intervals between each. Start with a 30–45 second rest interval, dropping to 20–30 and then to 10–20 seconds. Your effort level will determine whether you are doing an anaerobic threshold or VO$_2$ Max session. The harder the effort, the longer you are entitled to take as a rest interval.

After a 10 minute jog if you are doing a VO$_2$ Max session, five minutes if you are doing an anaerobic threshold session, repeat the set. In an anaerobic threshold session, the combined times for the 4 x 400 metres, less the rest intervals, should be 10 to 20 seconds less than your time for one mile in a race.

You can also do VO$_2$ Max and anaerobic threshold sessions on a treadmill. The principle is similar to the turbo-trainer sessions used in bicycle training, but in running you should take a slightly longer rest interval. Try: 10 minute warm-up at 50–75% (easy) effort. Then, do 45 seconds to 1:30 at 80% effort. Rest by jogging slowly for 45 seconds to 1:30. Repeat four times. Then jog easily for five to 10 minutes. Repeat the 4 x 45–1:30 set with 45–1:30 rest intervals. Finish by jogging gently to warm down.

Always remember to warm up before any training session. Jog, cycle or swim gently. Try to include some stretching in your warm ups. The harder the session, the more important the warm-up becomes.

Remember to gear your training toward the events you plan to do, both in terms of distance and terrain. If you know that your chosen triathlon has a hilly bike ride and a long descent at the end of the run, try to train on terrain that approximates those conditions.

In one session, you can incorporate all of the different types of training. Pepper a 30-mile bike ride with sprints between lampposts, and you've included sprint and distance training in one session. Indulge in a little speed-play, or *fartlek*: ride hard on an open, traffic-free stretch of road, then relax on the next stretch. Variety is the spice of life and the saviour of many a bored triathlete, too.

CHAPTER 5

A feel for the water

Swimming is probably the most technical of triathlon's component sports. While you can run without any semblance of grace and still beat the guy who glides along like a Greek god, it's unlikely that someone who flails about in the water will outpace the swimmer who slices neatly from one end of the pool to the other.

Some of us take to the water like ducks; others like gangsters wearing cement shoes. We can all improve our aquatic talents first by understanding the principles that help us to get through the water more quickly, then by developing a feel for the water and physically working to improve our swimming.

As a starting point, you should know that the front crawl is the preferred stroke of triathletes. Front crawl is the fastest of the four swimming strokes – the others are backstroke, breast-stroke and butterfly – because it uses primarily the upper body for propulsion, thus sparing the legs for later work in the bike and run sections. In addition, properly executed, it is a very efficient stroke. So, when we talk about swimming in this chapter, we are talking about front crawl.

Watch good swimmers in a pool. Note how their hands slice into the water, how they carry their elbows high on the recovery, how their body is streamlined and how they breathe in a relaxed manner. Good swimmers interact with the water; they have a feel for the water.

Something you might not notice immediately about good swimmers, but which also has a lot to do with their smooth style, is the way their hands move underwater. They don't push the water in a straight line from front to back: that's inefficient. If you were to push water in a straight line from front to back, you would not be able to find any traction from the water once it started moving. It's a bit like walking

The start of the 1987 Ironman. To be entitled to swim amongst these thrashing arms and legs you have to qualify for the race

52

Swim caps serve a dual purpose in
races: they help keep your head
warm during an open-water swim,
and make the job of identifying
and accounting for swimmers
much easier

up the down escalator, or swimming upstream. Good swimmers scull with their hands, making an S-like motion through the water. This way, they continually find still water, which gives them traction as they swim.

This is the same principle on which propellers operate, and propellers are the most efficient method known of moving an object through water. They are efficient because they move a large amount of water over a short distance. Propellers also create lift, using something called Bernoulli's principle. You may have heard of this in relation to aeroplanes: it is the principle that explains why a 747 can take off. Briefly, it works like this: an aeroplane wing is more highly cambered on its upper surface than the lower one. As the aeroplane increases speed for take-off, air travels quickly over the wings, and because of the camber of the wings, the air moves more quickly over the top surface. The resulting lower pressure on the upper surface when compared to the lower one leads to aerodynamic lift.

A boat's propeller employs the same principle. Its blades are pitched at an angle, and as the speed of the blades increases, unequal pressure on either side of the propeller forces its cargo forward.

Correctly pitched and using a sculling action, your hands will propel

Swimming is a very technical sport. One of the secrets to swimming well is high-elbow recovery, as shown here by Rob Barel in the Nice Triathlon

you through the water. They, too, are using the Bernoulli principle. If your hands are pitched correctly, you will cause water to travel more quickly over the back of the hand rather than over the palm, thus resulting in lift, which will propel you forward.

To further understand why pitch and a sculling action are preferable to a linear, paddle-wheel action, straddle a kickboard or lie on your back in the water. With your hands at your side, scull in the water, making small figure eight movements. Your hands are staying in one place in relation to your body, and yet you are moving forward. You can thank Mr Bernoulli.

Having looked at the principles that applied to your swimming should help you to move through the water more quickly and fluidly, you can now put them into practice.

The front crawl stroke can be broken down into different phases: the entry, catch, pull, exit and recovery.

Entry: this is the point where your hand enters the water. You should aim to slice into the water cleanly, pitching your hand at around 45 degrees to the surface, thumb and forefinger entering first. When the hand is in the water, you should reach forward, extending from your shoulders. *Exercise*: swim with hand paddles, concentrating on not slapping the water on entry. Hand paddles accentuate any stroke faults.

Catch: as you extend forward, rotate your forearm outward so that the palm turns from its diagonal entry position. Think about grabbing or catching the water, much

as you would grab a chin-up bar to pull yourself up to it. Think about maintaining a high elbow during the catch, your wrist should flex – this puts your hand in a good position to push water backwards. *Exercise*: catch-up drill, to accentuate your forward extension. Swim with both arms extended in front of you. Execute a complete stroke with one arm, but before the next arm takes its turn, allow both hands to meet in front of you. Concentrate on reaching out from the shoulders.

Pull: once you have caught your imaginary chin-up bar, you start to pull yourself up to it. As you start the pull, bend the elbow. Pressing downward with the arm, increase the bend in the elbow. Think about keeping the tip of your elbow pointing to the poolside and the palm toward the back of the pool. At the halfway point of the pull, your elbow should be bent at 90 degrees, and your fingertips should be lined up with or just over an imaginary line drawn down the centre of your body. Now, start to extend your lower arm and your wrist, so that the palm continues to face the back of the pool. Continue to extend your arm, moving it outwards, toward your hip, and extending your wrist so that you can exit the water cleanly with your hand, little finger first.

The pull phase ends when the palm is still facing the back of the pool; the recovery phase begins when you begin to turn your hand inwards, preparing to lift it cleanly from the water. *Exercise*: swim from one end of the pool to the other using one arm only. The non-working arm should be extended in front of you. Breathe every other stroke, and concentrate on all movements of the pull phase.

If your head position is correct in the water – the water just breaks around your hairline – you'll find that you are breathing in the bow wave you create when you swim

Recovery: with your hand now rotated so that the palm faces your thigh, slide your hand out of the water cleanly. The action is like taking your hand out of a trouser pocket. Remember: the pull ended before you removed your hand from the water. Don't exit the water with a hefty push of the hand. Lift your elbow upward and carry it forwards. Keep your elbow high and bent at all times during the recovery. If your elbow is too straight, you'll have excessive lateral movement, which will slow you down. Don't carry your hand too high during recovery and remember to keep your arm relaxed.

Exercise: to exaggerate high elbow recovery, drag your thumb along the side of your body when your arm is out of the water.

Kicking: while your arms do most of the work in the crawl stroke, you will still need to practise your kick from time to time. As a triathlete, you will be best served by something called the two-beat kick – one kick for every arm stroke – but when you train in the pool, you should practise a rapid flutter kick.

Don't be disheartened if you kick like fury and go nowhere. Just accept this as an illustration of how little the kick actually does propel you during the crawl stroke. Your kick will serve more as a rudder during races, and will help to keep your legs buoyant (something also helped by wetsuits) and can be useful when you want to sprint past someone. Otherwise, there is no use in losing sleep over a feeble kick.

Exercise: use a kickboard, draping your hands over the far end and lift your head out of the water. Or you can simply lie face-down in the water, body as streamlined as possible, arms extended in front of you. Now kick, using a breast-stroke arm action to lift your face out of the water when you want to breathe.

A good kick depends largely on ankle flexibility, which a lot of runners and cyclists are severely lacking. One way to enhance your ankle flexibility – and to make kick sessions go by more quickly – is to train with flippers. Make sure they are allowed at your pool first, though, as some do not allow them.

Breathing: should come naturally as you swim. You should be exhaling gently, with your face underwater, throughout the entry, catch and most of the pull phase. When you reach the halfway mark on the pull phase, start to exhale a little more vigorously. As your arm continues to work through the pull phase, start to turn your head to the side of the pulling arm. At the point where you finish the pull and start the recovery, your face should be out of the water, and you should be inhaling.

If you finish your exhalation with a good push of air through the mouth, just as it breaks the surface, water will be forced away from your lips, which should make inhaling easier.

The correct head position is very important if you want to breathe efficiently. If you carry your head too high in the water, then you will find that your mouth is in the bow wave you create when you swim. If the water hits your head at the hairline (assuming you are not receding . . .) you should be able to turn your head and breathe at the bottom of the bow wave. In addition holding your head too high will

cause your legs to drop, making you less streamlined and therefore slower.

On each arm cycle, your body will roll 35 to 45 degrees, more on the side on which you are breathing. This is a natural action and should be neither forced nor inhibited.

Inhalation should occur when the body is at its maximum roll, or when the hand begins the recovery phase. Too late, and you will be forcing your face deeper in the water than you want it by the action of your arms.

It is not uncommon to see many swimming debutantes attempting to get from one end of the pool to the other without breathing. This is not natural and only makes swimming more difficult. *Exercise*: bilateral breathing is useful not only in equalising body roll, but will also come in handy when you need to navigate in open-water swims. Bilateral breathing means, as the name suggests, breathing on both sides, every third stroke.

The 30-minute swim

When you swim above a certain speed, your muscles produce lactic acid faster than your energy production system can resynthesise it. This causes blood lactate to build up to painful levels, which in turn makes you slow down to recover.

The point at which you can no longer synthesize lactic acid quickly enough is your anaerobic threshold. Working at your anaerobic threshold you can sustain a constant pace for 20-30 minutes without having to slow down significantly to recover from lactic acid build up. It is important to train your body to tolerate different levels of work.

If your wetsuit obstinately clings to your ankles, try dabbing some petroleum jelly on the problem spots before the swim

A good wetsuit is designed to help you get out of it quickly. Start removing it as soon as you stand up after the swim section

Open water swimming

The previous section was all about perfecting your technique in the pool, but when you start triathlon, you are likely to encounter a new animal: the open water swim.

Open water swimming differs enormously from pool swimming. The water is usually colder, especially in northern countries. There are no black lines on the bottom of the sea or a lake. There is a tide, and troublesome waves. There will be a lot of people kicking, and arms flailing, trying to get in front of you during an open water swim.

It is at the start of the swim, when you are battling in the mêlée of elbows and feet that you will probably ask

The start of the swim in any triathlon always sees a mad dash for the best position in the water. Make sure you have seeded yourself wisely, or the good swimmers will swim over, under or around you

After a sea swim, spend sufficient time under the shower to get rid of the salt water on your skin, as otherwise it will only cause discomfort on the bike and run sections

yourself, 'What am I doing here?' But once you get going and find your rhythm, an open water swim can be quite enjoyable.

What you need for open water swimming

Triathlon's rules allow you to wear a wetsuit. Sometimes, they will even insist that you **do** wear a wetsuit – when the water temperature drops below a certain point. At other times, in the Hawaii Ironman for instance, you won't need to or want to wear a wetsuit as the water is warm and

buoyant enough.

If you have the means, invest in a full wetsuit made specifically for swimming. That means full-length legs, which will help you to keep the lower half of your body buoyant without too much kicking; sufficient shoulder movement to facilitate a good crawl stroke; the right kind of neoprene to minimise what's called frictional drag, ie the drag caused by friction between the skin, or your wetsuit, and the water; a correct fit to your body; and a good construction that allows easy removal after the swim. Such makes of wetsuit are Quintana Roo, Gul,

Water under the bridge: competitors in the 1992 Bath Triathlon face the race's first discipline

61

Entry: with a high elbow and relaxed shoulder movement, slice cleanly into the water with your hand tilted at 45 degrees. Then extend forward from the shoulder

Recovery: this is the phase when you breathe and turn to the same side as your recovering arm. Remember to carry your elbow high, keeping the arm relaxed from shoulder to fingertips

Terrapin and Aquaman, among others.

Put a dab of petroleum jelly on the parts of your body where the wetsuit is likely to rub – the neck, shoulders, armpits – and around the ankles to facilitate its removal. If your wetsuit has a zip down the back, tie a long piece of cord to the zip. It's frustrating looking for that little zip tag when you've just left the water. With the cord in place, you can reach behind you, grab, pull and divest.

You will also be required by the rules to wear a swim cap, which will usually serve a treble purpose of classifying you according to age group or sex, making you easier to spot in the water, and keeping your head warm. Swim caps, which come in either Lycra or rubber, also reduce friction drag. If you suffer from the cold and the race organiser supplies you with a Lycra swim cap, wear a rubber one underneath. Always wear the swim cap supplied by the race organiser.

Goggles will help to make your open water swim more enjoyable. Buy goggles that do not fog up, that cut out the glare on the surface of the water, and that fit your face without leaking. You might find a fairly cheap pair of goggles adequate for your needs, or you might want to invest in a pair of £100.00 Swans. It's up to you. But do test them before the race.

What you won't be allowed to use during an open water swim are pullbuoys, flippers or hand-paddles.

Navigating during an open water swim is not as easy as swimming up and down in a pool. You will have to take note of and recognise landmarks before you enter the water. Stand at the start and finish of the course and take careful note of things like lighthouses, piers, beachside snackbars, anything that helps you to recognise the area and get your bearings. **Don't** use boats as landmarks. They tend to move.

If it's at all possible, do a recce of the swim course with another swimmer a couple of days before the race. Go round the course at an easy pace, taking note of landmarks, turns, potential difficulties, etc. Don't swim for time, and don't swim alone.

The course is likely to be a loop. Your landmarks could change from your normal breathing side to the other. In addition, the direction from which the tide comes could well change. This is a good reason to perfect bilateral breathing.

To help you navigate, it is also worthwhile learning to breathe and

A good pair of goggles is an essential part of a triathlete's wardrobe. If you swim in salt water, rinsing your goggles in fresh water afterwards will help to prolong their life

Different phases of the crawl stroke: the swimmer in the foreground is at full extension of the entry phase and starting the catch phase. The middle lane swimmer has just slid his hand out of the water for the recovery phase. The swimmer in the background is pulling with his arm underwater, bent at 90 degrees; the other arm is prepared for entry

spot check in front of you simultaneously. Practise this in the pool, and use it in open water swims: every fifth or sixth stroke, lift your head and look to the front to check that you are going in the right direction. To facilitate this, flatten your hand entry slightly. Try not to over-compensate for the raised head position with a furious kick, as this will only serve to tire your legs unnecessarily. Once you

have got your bearings, return to your normal swimming style. During a race, top triathletes raise their heads and spot check every five or six strokes.

Another tip to help you to check your position is to swim water polo style, ie with the head out of the water for a couple of strokes.

You can, of course, follow other swimmers – unless you are at the very front, in which case you can follow the lead boat. But remember that they might be poor navigators. It still pays to spot check every once in a while.

By sitting on another swimmer's feet, you can legally draft during the swim section. You will derive the same benefits as you do from drafting on a bike, which is illegal in triathlon. The swimmer in front of you will drag you along at his or her pace, and you invest less effort.

If the water temperature is cold, be prepared for it to take your breath away initially. This is another good reason to swim the course beforehand – so that you can grow accustomed to the initial shock. Don't panic over the sensation. It will pass. If, for some reason, it doesn't, you would be wise to postpone your triathlon efforts to another day.

If you ever get in trouble during a swim, roll onto your back and raise one arm out of the water to attract attention. If you pass a swimmer who appears to be in difficulty, stop to help them. Their life is more important than your race.

Always seed yourself for an open water swim start. Don't position yourself at the front of the pack just for the chance to say that you started with Mark Allen or Glenn Cook. The top swimmers will swim over, under, around and across you. Glenn Cook told me once that people have tried to grab his wetsuit and flip him over during swims. You need to be strong enough to put up with those kinds of shenanigans, and fast enough to get away from their perpetrators if you are planning to start at the front of the pack.

It's also not a good idea to start right at the back, however, as you are likely to encounter a group of breast-strokers. A breast-stroke kick taken between the eyes or even in the back is a powerful and painful thing. Sarah Springman was forced to abandon the Nice Triathlon one year when a breast-stroker connected with her bottom during the swim, causing deep bruising. I'll never forget Springman sitting at the roadside in the Alpes Maritimes, on the brink of tears, massaging her cheek and saying in that inimitable Springman way, 'I think this is the most disappointing moment in my triathlon career.'

As you near the end of an open water swim, prepare yourself for the transition from swimming to cycling. This transition starts when you stop swimming and stand up to leave the water. You could experience dizziness not dissimilar to that created when you get out of bed too quickly. This isn't unusual, and is due to the fact that you have just spent a period of time in a horizontal position and are now upright, and because the blood pumping through your arms during the swim is now being channelled toward your legs. You should pull out of this dizzy phase, if indeed you experience it at all, within seconds.

With the swim over, you can start to tear at your wetsuit the minute you are upright and on the way out of the water. If you've just finished a salt-water swim, have a shower on the way to the bike – the organisers will usually have made provisions for it. If the water was very cold, take time to warm up again.

The more open water swims you do, the less frightening they become. Even if, years after your first rough and tumble swim start, you still find yourself asking, 'What am I doing here?' take heart. You're not alone. Keep swimming, and it will pass.

Sarah's cold water hell

In the early days of triathlon in Britain, we had training camps in the southwest in winter, and Aleck Hunter, a man whose unbridled enthusiasm for the sport hit you the minute you met him, made us go into water that was less than 15°C. Intending to go in for one or two minutes, we would stay in for five or ten, coming out totally hypothermic. I never realised, when I was turning purple in that water, that in an odd way it was going to serve me well one day: it left me hardened in mind and body to the idea of the two-mile swim at the National Long Course Championships at Holme Pierrepont in 1985.

The weather had been awful leading up to the race. I didn't sleep much the night before, but that was to be expected as I was defending the title I had won in Durham the year before. In addition there was this unknown woman from Zimbabwe on the starting line. She was

The right amount of body roll is critical for a good front crawl stroke. With practise it will come naturally and shouldn't be too pronounced

Paula Newby-Fraser and 1985 was her first year in triathlon.

We were to start with the two-mile swim. Then there was something a little over 50 miles on the bike, followed by five laps of a three-mile run circuit. Around 200 people entered the race, about 150 started and only about 50 to 60 of us finished the swim.

None of the leaders was really aware of the carnage that was going on around us, with people swimming to the side and packing. All the pictures in the papers the next day weren't about the people who had won the race, but about the craziness of the whole event. It was not good publicity for triathlon, and it forced a rethink by the British Triathlon Association as to whether or not swim distances should be cut in extreme weather conditions for safety reasons.

I came out of the swim tenth woman. Paula was in front of me, and I caught her about halfway into the bike ride. She stayed close to me, until I managed to put in a bit of a spurt and get away. After that, I took quite a lot of time out of her on the bike. I finished the bike section in fourth place . . . overall.

There was a big screen at Holme Pierrepont, where all the spectators who had come to watch the event could see exactly what was going on. The result of the bike section flicked onto the screen: in front of me were Bernie Shrosbree, a Royal Marine, Glenn Cook, and a third male competitor whose name I can no longer recall. When my name appeared in fourth place, people thought the screen was simply showing the leader of the women's race. When it was confirmed that I was fourth overall, the crowd went absolutely wild.

The reception I got in the transition area between the bike and run was unforgettable. And on each of the five laps of Holme Pierrepont, when I passed through the start-finish area, I got a huge cheer. I finished seventh overall.

It was a good race for me but not a very good race for triathlon. And Holme Pierrepont 1985 was the last time I beat Paula Newby-Fraser.

CHAPTER 6

Cycling

Cycling is triathlon's second event. It will – or should, unless you're a terrible swimmer or runner – take up more of your time during races than the swim or run sections, and cycle training too, will take up much of your time.

On the bike, you are trying to achieve maximum speed by the most efficient means possible. Mechanical considerations play nearly as important a role in achieving this end as the intelligent training you will be putting in to improve your performance.

Step one is to buy a bike that is right for you. Go to a specialist shop or to a frame-builder if you have the wherewithal to invest in a custom-built bike. In very basic terms, the frame size you will be looking for will be equal to the measurement of your inside leg in inches, minus ten. Take this measurement standing in stocking feet, and measuring from the groin right down to the floor. If, for example,

you have an inside leg measurement of 31, your bike frame size should be 21 inches. If the size you arrive at doesn't correlate with an available frame size, round *down* to the nearest size, not up.

Next, check the length of the top tube. You don't want to be hunched up on the bike. This is especially relevant to you as a triathlete, as you will have to run after cycling, and a tube that's too short will lead to lower back problems. Too long a tube will make you stretch out, and you will probably experience shoulder and upper back problems. To check that your top tube is the right size for you, place your elbow at the tip of the saddle and extend your forearm toward the handlebars. There should be about two inches between your fingertips and the handlebars.

You should also sit on the bike that you intend to buy – before you buy it – and see if you feel comfortable with it. With the help of the shop assistant, adjust the saddle height so that, when you are sitting on the saddle with the heel of your foot on the pedals at six o'clock, the knee of your extended leg is slightly bent. Adjust the fore/aft position of your saddle so that, when your pedals are parallel to the ground your knee lines up roughly with the centre of your pedal. Check this by dangling a weight on the end of a string and hold the other end against the small bone on the outside of the knee. The weight should hang level with the centre of the pedal. There is room for manoeuvre on both these positions, but they are useful guidelines.

Another consideration when buying a bike is handlebar width. You can change handlebar widths, and if you are a petite woman, you probably won't want the wide handlebars that come as stock fittings on standard road racing bikes. The right fit of conventional handlebar should allow you to sit with your hands on the brake hoods or drops with your hands and arms no wider than shoulder width apart.

Finding the right bars

Lennard Zinn is a custom frame builder, and has studied bicycle aerodynamics. He shares his technical expertise and gives his advice on the use of aero-bars.

Aero-bars were borne when Boone Lennon, inventor of the original Scott DH bar, came up with a design which brings the rider's arms closer together, promoting a narrower riding position

Part of the aim behind triathlon, or aero-bars, is to bring the forearms as close together as possible. This should not be done at the cost of comfort or safety

which mimics a downhill skier's position. This does not mean that all of the attainable or desirable narrowness will immediately be achieved simply by fitting such handlebars – you must still work on your body position. And the one factor that has been found to consistently produce less drag in wind-tunnel tests is keeping the elbows closer together to attain a narrower position.

The ideal aerodynamic position is created by having the inside of the forearms touching along their entire length, but this forfeits control. So ideally, you should aim to bring your hands as close together as possible to achieve the most aerodynamic position without sacrificing control.

If narrowness is next to godliness in achieving maximum speed, then maintaining a low profile follows close behind. You should aim to have a position in which your back is horizontal and flat. This is usually achieved by lowering or lengthening the bike's stem and stretching the back out. It was found in wind-tunnel tests that by lowering the handlebars, which results in a flatter back, you can cut your drag factor significantly.

You might find that your knees bang on your chest when riding in this low position. To overcome this, slide the saddle forward, opening the angle between your thigh and torso, and allowing more knee to chest clearance. Chest clearance should be barely maintained without arching the back or bowing the knees outwards which creates drag. The stem will most likely need to be lengthened to maintain your

flat-back position. It will take time to get used to riding in a low, flat back and narrow arm position, so be prepared to practise.

Some triathletes favour radically far-forward positions on the bike, but it is possible to find a good aerodynamic position without placing yourself too far forward. In addition, by moving from the minimimally forward position necessary for chest clearance to the far-forward positions adopted by some triathletes, there is a 20% drop in power output. It's better to work down gradually through less aerodynamic positions while maintaining leg power than to sacrifice power for speed. On the other hand the far forward position is thought to facilitate the bike to run transition. Still, losing 20% power on the bike will usually cost you more time than you'd gain by a smooth, fast transition.

If you don't naturally adopt the optimal position on your bike, you are likely to be slower when riding with aero-bars than a cyclist with a naturally good position riding on ordinary drop handlebars. If you are uncomfortable in the optimum position, you will be constantly adjusting it, probably to one that is more upright and wider, which creates more wind drag. Every movement of your body will reorganise the air flow around you, creating turbulence.

Far-forward positions rapidly gained acceptance in the triathlon world because any athlete who was new to cycling could immediately achieve an aerodynamic position with a flat back by greatly decreasing the angle between

Mark Allen's position
using aero-bars is
exemplary. Note his
flat back and narrow
forearm position. No
wonder he wins so
many triathlons

Paula Newby-Fraser's 24-inch
wheeled Hamilton Sattui bike is an

HED wheels have
shown in tests to be
the most aerodynamic
available. Triathletes
helped to make them
popular

Mark Allen keeps a relaxed grip on
his aero-bars whilst holding his
rivals in a vice-like grip of speed
and determination. He's on his
way to another win in Nice, 1991

the thigh and torso. It was simpler and quicker than training the body to accept a flatter, more stretched-out position. However, tri- and duathletes who adopted these positions early on now find that they can increase their power while maintaining a low, flat-back position when their saddle is positioned further back. They have trained their bodies in a non-classical way to ride comfortably in a low, flat position.

Duathlete Kenny Souza, for example, after a wind-tunnel test in 1990, ended up with his saddle about eight centimetres further back than the position he used in 1989. He was able to generate higher power output in the new position, and he also says that he was climbing better.

You can make big improvements in your cycling position by focusing on pelvic positioning. Many triathletes have their pelvis rotated back, causing their stomach to crease and bulge out and their lower back to arch. Consequently, they are unable to support their weight effectively, even in a high, tourist position. They also tend to experience difficulty riding in a low position. If you were to ride in a low position without addressing the problem of pelvic rotation, you would be unable to hold form over any length of time. The result would be to relax into a less effective position at the expense of your speed.

With the pelvis rotated forward and down, you will have better leg extension and smoother, unconfined pedalling. Your pedal stroke is not

Cycling will demand a large part of your training time and choosing pleasant routes to train on will help that time to pass quickly

contracted at the top of its rotation, which means you could ride with a higher saddle position than an average cyclist with the same leg length as you. This is an important consideration for triathletes, as a higher saddle position is thought to facilitate the bike to run transition. A forward pelvic rotation also allows for a flat back, even in a very low position, and it allows you to stretch out farther and lower, helping your pedal power.

Equipment has come a long way since the early days and the bike industry has benefited in technical terms from the advent of aero-bars and disc wheels

It isn't yet possible to say what angle of handlebar tilt is optimal. Select a bar tilt that allows you to assume a comfortable pedalling position. This will probably also be the fastest position for you.

Wheels and pedals

A basic road bike will come with 700C spoked wheels. Today, it is possible to buy triathlon bikes with smaller wheels, for example, a Quintana Roo or Hamilton Sattui with 26- and 24-inch wheels respectively. The principle is that smaller wheels are more aerodynamic, but they do have more rolling resistance. The geometry – that is, the seat and head angles – and componentry set-up on these bikes will be different to a conventional road

bike's. You cannot simply buy a bike built to take 700C wheels and slap on 24-inchers. It won't work.

You can also invest in so-called tri-spoke wheels or disc wheels, more aerodynamic than a conventional spoked wheel. Take note, however: there are times when a disc wheel will hinder you on the bike – on a course with strong side winds, for instance. And while tri-spoke wheels can be used on the front and back of a bike, discs are intended only for the back.

Wheels are quite a fragile part of a bike, tending to buckle and sometimes even crack when they hit large potholes. Ruining a pair of expensive tri-spoke wheels is infinitely more painful than buckling your 700Cs. The best solution is to have two sets of wheels – one for training and one for racing. Take both sets to races, so that you have the choice of using the wheels which best suit the course and climactic conditions.

Pedals are also worth more than a glancing thought when you're buying your bike. Many triathlon bikes are fitted with clipless pedals. They were rapidly adopted by users of clips and straps, which necessitate reaching down and tightening a leather or plastic strap which encircles the pedal, passing through a toeclip on top. By tightening the strap, the foot is held in place on the pedal, and the rider can pull up on the pedal as well as pressing down – one of the secrets behind effective pedalling. Most clipless pedals eliminate the need to reach down and pull on a strap, although there are some older makes that require you to release a lever on the pedal to free your foot. Remember that any extraneous movement on the bike creates turbulence and therefore makes you less aerodynamic. Clipless pedals also eliminate the possibility of cutting off circulation in the foot when the strap is pulled too tight. A well-adjusted clipless pedal will allow a quick release simply by twisting your foot laterally.

As with all other bike equipment, clipless pedals have evolved over the years, and you can now get certain pedals that allow more foot movement than the original click-ins.

Once your feet are in the pedals, the aim should be to achieve a smooth pedalling action. When you pedal, think of circles, not an up and down action. Drive down your heel, scraping imaginary chewing gum off the bottom of your shoe at the bottom of the pedalling action, and then pull up on the pedal, all in a smooth, flowing, circular action.

Saddles and seatposts

Innovations in triathlon have touched even the humble seatpost and seatposts which curve forward have evolved. This places the saddle in a forward position and thereby tilts the triathlete's pelvis, which can assist their pedalling technique. Tests have shown, however, that some triathletes have their saddles too far forward, and are, in fact, losing power.

A conventional seatpost is perfectly adequate, of course, if your position on the bike is good to start with. Aerodynamic seatposts are available – they have an elliptical circumference, rather than round.

Your saddle should be chosen primarily for comfort, but you should also consider that you will probably have a wet bottom for part of the time you spend on your bike. Choose a saddle made of a material that won't become sodden or slippery when wet. Good, old-fashioned leather works well for triathlon saddles.

The frame

Conventionally, bike frames are made from steel, a durable, forgiving material. It is easy to work with and bike manufacturers can put together a perfectly adequate frame at a very acceptable cost using steel. Frames made of alternative materials such as aluminium, titanium, or carbon fibre are usually lighter, but also tend to cost more. Aluminium frames are less shock absorbent than steel ones. Carbon fibre frames are sometimes made in a mould – known as a monocoque frame – and should be checked for proper alignment.

Triathlon has helped the humble bicycle to evolve in recent years into a very high-tech machine. Thanks to the sport we now have aero-bars, tri-spoke wheels and behind the saddle bottle cages. All of these innovations are designed to help you to go faster, and they do so by making you more aerodynamic. By trimming weight here and there on the bike, you will also improve your speed.

Comfort on the bike is also very important: to achieve maximum comfort, you should ensure that your bike is set up to fit your physique, and you should also wear the right clothes.

Clothing for training

Hot weather: Coolmax jersey, shorts with good chamois lining.

Cool weather: jersey with thermal top underneath, shorts as above.

Cold weather: thermal top against the skin, jersey over it, windproof jacket. Warm, fleecy full-length tights with chamois. Socks, shoes and overshoes.

Wet weather: add a waterproof but breathable cycling jacket, eg Frank Shorter Goretex jacket.

Clothing for racing

Triathlon top and shorts with quick-drying chamois. In a long triathlon, such as the Ironman, you would be better off wearing your most comfortable cycling gear, ie shorts with a real chamois leather lining. The seconds lost by changing from your swimming gear into your cycling gear, as opposed to wearing the same kit throughout the triathlon, are usually compensated for by a more comfortable ride.

Always wear a helmet. It must be Snell or ANSI approved. Helmets are obligatory in races.

Eyeshades: either tinted or clear. Not only do they protect against glare and the sun's harmful rays, but they also stave off bugs and other flying objects. Choose a pair made from shatterproof material.

Gloves: protect your hands in the event of a crash and also help to avoid blisters and discomfort.

Sunscreen: essential for palefaces. There is new type of cancer on the upswing, which has been dubbed cyclists' melanoma, for the obvious reason that cyclists who regularly expose unprotected skin to the sun are susceptible to it. You will acquire a healthy golden tan, albeit a bit more slowly, wearing sunscreen, and you will be cutting down on the risks associated with excessive exposure to the sun.

Technique

There are some basic lessons in cycling technique to be learned, in addition to the more advanced food for thought offered in the next section:

1 Cornering

Try to cut corners by taking a straight line across the road, but be aware of traffic and never cross over the central dividing line. As you approach the corner, stop pedalling and lean into the corner. Your inside leg should be raised, knee bent and pointing into the corner. The outside leg should be

The bike section of a
triathlon should be like
a time trial. It's a time
to be alone with
yourself, your thoughts
and the effort of the race

When the profile of a
course starts to climb,
get out of the saddle to
help yourself up the hill

straight and pressing onto its pedal. As you come out of the corner, you can begin pedalling. Good cornering skills will help you tremendously on hilly, twisting courses.

2 Gearing

People will talk to you about gear tables, but it is unlikely that you are going to calculate that, on the next hill, the most effective gearing will be X inches. More helpful than being able to spout figures is to know how different gear combinations work. Your bike is probably going to come fitted with a 42/52 tooth chainset at the front, and a rear block which is easily changeable, with anything from six to eight different rings, each with anything from 11 to over 30 teeth. The hardest gear to push – the biggest in gear table inches – is engaged when you shift onto the big ring at the front and the smallest at the back. The easiest gear engages the small ring at the front and the biggest at the back. You will probably be doing most of your training in gears between 42/15 and 42/19, depending on your development as a cyclist. (In gear table terms, that's between 60 and 75 inches.) You should be spinning the pedals at a high cadence – between 90 to 110 rpm – so that you are working your cardiovascular system and your legs, without putting too great a strain on the knees.

Young triathletes should be especially vigilant not to push too big a gear. In fact a chainring no bigger than 42 teeth should be fitted to young

triathletes' bikes, so that the temptation of cranking out the miles in a monster gear is eliminated. It is still possible to win bike races and triathlons riding a small gear, and it's the best possible way to learn good cycling habits.

You can change both your chainwheel and your rear blocks. Some professional cyclists use a 53/39 combination on the front. You can use a small cluster – a rear block that goes

Back in the early days of aero-bars, everyone coveted Scott DH bars, but they were not without drawbacks. These curvaceous bars were not sturdy or ideal for climbing; needless to say they have evolved a lot since then

Almost the ultimate triathlon bike . . . aero-bars, shifters on the extensions, a tri-spoke front wheel and rear disc wheels

from 12 to 19 teeth, for instance – on a flat course, or you might opt for a wider range of gears on a rolling or hilly course.

3 Hill climbing

Anticipate the hill. Change into an easier gear before you start to climb. If you are going to climb in the saddle rest your hands, so that they stay relaxed, on the tops of the handlebars.

If you are going to get out of the saddle, wrap your hands around your brake levers and pull up on the bars as you climb. If you have full aero-bars as opposed to clip-ons, pull up on the bars' drops. Watch pro-cyclists when they climb: when in the saddle their upper bodies are virtually stock still; when out of the saddle, they rock their bikes back and forth to help them get up the hill.

Rules and regulations

There are a couple of simple rules to follow during the bike section of a triathlon:

1 You must wear a helmet and it must be Snell or ANSI approved. Snell and ANSI approvals are marked inside the helmet shell on a small sticker. Popular makes of helmet which carry such approval are Bell, Giro, Specialized, and Vetta, to name a few.

2 You may not draft by sitting on someone else's wheel. It is so effective in reducing the effort/effect ratio that you can sometimes see Tour de France riders cruising along in the middle of the pack at 25 mph without pedalling.

Triathlon is an individual sport. The bike section is intended to be a time trial. If you are overtaken by another cyclist, you should drop back to the distance that is allowed by the rules. If you are the overtaker, you should pass your rider cleanly and quickly, without sitting on their wheel. The precise rules on drafting are outlined in Chapter 15.

If you choose to draft, bear in mind that what you are doing is not only the act of a cheat, but that your dishonesty

Good cornering technique is essential if you want to avoid more than your fair share of scrapes with the tarmac. The inside pedal should be raised, the knee pointing slightly outward. The outside leg should be straight, with weight applied to the pedal

could also have disastrous effects on someone else's race.

Drafting: a high price to pay

Sarah on drafting

After a disappointing European Middle Distance Championships in Stein, Holland, in 1988, I was really determined when I got to the Olympic Distance Championships in Venice. A week before the race, I had a brilliant training session, running 17:21 for 5km. That on top of excellent cycling results – I was third in the Best British All Rounders Series, won the bronze medal in the National 100-mile Time Trial Championships, came fourth in the National Track Pursuit Championship, and I won the National Long Course Championships for the fifth time in a row. I also beat my biggest British rival, Sarah Coope, quite decisively at the Paris Triathlon a week before Venice.

In Venice, I started as favourite, and I knew I could win. I was light and running brilliantly, clocking about 35 minutes for 10km. I reckoned it was going to be pretty tough for any of the women there to cope with: and so it proved.

When I arrived in Venice, everything seemed a bit disorganised. I managed to suss out the course and realised that the route for the bike ride was going to be a little crowded. We all made suggestions that they could slightly adjust the route, but nobody paid any attention. When I saw the swim course being marked out on the morning of the race, I said to Robin Brew, an ex-international swimmer and member of Britain's national triathlon team, that it looked short to me. He agreed,

saying that what should have been a 1500-metre course appeared to be only 1200 metres long.

I had a good swim though, and I think I went into the lead of the women's race within the first three or four kilometres on the bike. Even by that stage, huge packs were forming; people I had passed came past me again, sitting on the wheel of other people. I had to let them go, because I didn't want to draft. I desperately wanted to win the race, but I wasn't prepared to do so by cheating.

When I saw Sarah Coope and Cathy Bow sitting by the side of the road because they'd decided they didn't want to have anything to do with the race, I slowed and thought about stopping. But then I remembered Stein and my inability to finish there, and I decided I had to finish in Venice. I thought: 'Maybe they'll disqualify people who draft here, but I'm going to finish and see where I come.'

Three groups have responsibility for a race; first, the European Triathlon Union, for sanctioning the race. They were all there well before the start of the race. They had ample time to insist that the organiser change the course. Then, there's the race organiser who neither had an effective course nor drafting marshals to check the situation. The short swim exacerbated the problem, as everyone was close together coming out of the water.

Soon, a lot of the women who had been drafting dropped off the back of their packs, and I managed to pass them again. Finishing the bike ride, I expected the leaders to be three or four minutes ahead of me, because they'd shot past so quickly at the beginning. But in fact the leader was only 1:40 up. Given how well I was running, I knew the win was possible.

He could almost be a triathlete! Greg LeMond legitimised aero-bars – note his flat back and narrow forearm position

There is some debate as to whether
drafting should be allowed in the
sport. Until a decision is taken
there are some rules governing how
close one rider can be to another
during a race

I set off like a madwoman. By halfway, I was in third place, but the others were in my sight. I was motivated by total disgust at the way they had behaved and the desire to prove that, even if they did draft, I was still the best. I passed the last two at six and seven kilometres and won by about 19 seconds.

Immediately after the race, I was handed a microphone and laid into those who had shamelessly cheated. While I was talking, an announcement came over the public address system: the race result was nullified, and our European titles had gone up in smoke – Rob Barel was the winner of the men's race.

The guilty party was the athletes. They didn't have to draft. The way they chose to race was up to them. Unfortunately, many of them wanted to cheat, and unfortunately, their thoughtless actions cost Rob and me the titles we fought fairly and squarely for in Venice.

CHAPTER 7

Running

Running is the most natural of all triathlon's sports, in the sense that most of us start running as children and continue to run throughout the course of our lives, if only to avoid missing a bus. In triathlon terms, it can also be the most difficult sport. When you start the run you already have a swim and bike leg behind you. You hop off the bike, your leg muscles having done a couple of hours of one type of work, and you ask them to do essentially the opposite. If you've never experienced the bike to run transition in a triathlon, you are in for a treat.

As natural an activity as running may be, there are still some basic rules of technique to follow. When you run, concentrate on the following points of technique:

1 Lean forward slightly. Look at the postures of top distance runners, and you'll see that they all lean forward about five per cent. To help yourself to achieve this, try fixing your gaze on a spot on the ground about 10 to 15 metres in front of you.

2 Strike the ground lightly with your heel first. Your feet should point fairly straight ahead when you run. If you were to slow down the foot action of a runner, you would see that he or she lands on the heel and then rolls forward, through the ball of the foot, pushing off with the toes. A normal footfall sees the runner neither gravitating too far to the outside of the foot (supination) nor toward the inside (pronation). If you do tend to pronate or supinate, don't be alarmed. You are not alone, and running shoe manufacturers tuned into that fact years ago and now produce shoes for runners with either tendency.

The best way to determine if you pronate or supinate is to get an experienced runner to watch you run. Another way is to examine the wear on the soles of old running shoes. In fact, to help the shop assistants to give you sound advice on which shoes to buy, take an old pair of running shoes with you when you buy your next pair.

Mark Allen's long, easy stride has helped him to win many a triathlon. Traditionally, Allen comes from behind on the run section to win races. If he comes off the bike in the lead there's no hope at all for the rest of the field

3 At the beginning of the run section, keep your stride short. Too long a stride incorporates a high kick at the back of the stride, which tires the hamstring muscles. As your legs begin to loosen up on the run, lengthen your stride, but not excessively. Your gait should be natural and flowing. Don't shuffle, but don't run like a prancing horse.

4 Use your arms: you will be surprised how much your arms work during a run. On hills, you pump with your arms to help you crest the summit. At the end of a run, concentrating on working with your upper body as well as your legs can get you past the competition and across the line before them. Sometimes, if you haven't run for a long time, your arms will be more tired than your legs when you take up the sport again!

Your hands, arms and shoulders should be relaxed but working when you run. The hands and forearms shouldn't cross over the body as they swing back and forth during the run. Nor should they be held too high, a problem many women have. If you carry your hands too high, try running with them at your side for 20 steps during your running session. Then, bend the arms slightly at the elbow. If you are used to carrying your arms too high, you will now feel that they are too low. They probably aren't. Try to maintain this position throughout the run, repeating the steps when you sense that your hands are rising again.

Don't tense your hands into a fist. To avoid this, try running with your hands held open. If the desire to make a fist is overwhelming, touch your middle finger to your thumb.

Don't hunch your shoulders, something many a runner does when tired. If you feel tension in your shoulders during a run, do a few arm circles.

5 Keep your breathing relaxed. Breathe from your diaphragm, not from your chest. You should be able to breathe without moving your upper body. Think of the wall of your stomach as a bellows: when it bulges outward, it is sucking in air; when it pushes inwards, it is forcing air out of your lungs.

Choosing your shoes

Your running kit only need be basic. All you need is a good pair of shoes and socks, shorts or tights, and a vest or thermal top, depending on the season. Remember the following when you are buying your running shoes:

1 They should be suited to your style of running. Are you a pronator or supinator? Heavy or lightweight? Do you land hard on your heel or are you a midfoot striker?

2 What terrain do you intend to train and race on? If you train mainly on trails, then you will need shoes that grip and support well, that cushion against the shock from stones, roots, etc. You will probably be racing on the road, however, in which case you will most likely need a different shoe. Some shoes serve both purposes, but there is no harm in having separate pairs of training and racing shoes. Just make sure you break in the racing shoes during a training run, before you actually race.

3 Buy running shoes about half a size bigger than you would buy your normal walking shoes. When you run, your feet bang against the front of your running shoes, and this can result in lost toenails. In addition, during long races, and especially

Your running sessions needn't – indeed shouldn't – see you pounding tarmac without cease. Off-road running develops your reaction times and is also less jarring on your joints

in the heat, your feet will swell during a run.

4 Remember that running shoes have a shelf-life. Using shoes beyond their shelf-life can contribute to running injuries. An average pair of running shoes worn by an average mileage runner should last between three and six months. Even if you can't visually detect excessive wear, the EVA mid-sole – the portion between the sole of your shoe and the shoe's upper – will compress significantly after three to six months' use, diminishing the shock absorbency of your shoes.

Socks, shorts and vests

Try to buy 100% cotton or Coolmax socks. Double lined socks can help to prevent blisters. Avoid those with seams across the toes.

Shorts and vests made of new generation synthetics such as the latest polypropylene brands are better than unblended cotton. These fabrics wick perspiration away from the skin and allow it to evaporate quickly from the material, leaving you cooler and without that perspiration-sodden feeling that 100% cotton can give you. Lycra, too, tends to dry quickly, but doesn't have the wicking properties of hollow fibres.

In winter, thermal fabrics serve the same purpose, transporting perspiration away from the skin. Dress warmly, in layers, with a thermal layer next to your skin. Gloves are a useful addition to a winter running wardrobe, as is a lightweight hat.

Goal Pace Sessions

First select the pace that you would realistically like to run for 10 kilometres. Remember that you will run a 10 kilometre road race faster than you will run 10km in a triathlon. So, if you can run 10 kilometres on the road in 50 minutes but need 52 minutes in a triathlon, settle for 51 minutes, or 5.1 minutes per kilometre, as your goal for these sessions. Now go the 800 metre column in the table and note down the time in which you should run 800 metres plus your rest interval from the adjacent column.

If the time in your 800 metre column is greater than three hours 15 minutes, go to the 600 metre column. Note the time in which you should run 600 metres and your rest interval.

The session will consist of six to eight x 800-metre or six to eight x 600-metre intervals. Work to the times given in the table, with the appropriate rest intervals. Always warm up and warm down.

If you run a 10km road race in 50 minutes and it takes you 52 minutes in a triathlon, you might choose as your goal a 51-minute 10km run and your session would look like this:

1 Warm up by stretching and jogging easily for one or two miles – four to eight laps of a 400 metre track.

2 Do six to eight x 600 metres in three hours four minutes with 61 seconds rest intervals.

3 Warm down by jogging four to eight laps of the track and stretching afterwards.

Training, stress and rest

Running is the most stressful of triathlon's sports. Overdo the running training, and you will also run into difficulties such as shin splints, stress fractures, and fatigue, to name just a few of the pitfalls. Monitor your training and your body's reaction to it, and give yourself time to recover from each training session.

The muscles of marathon runners suffer significant trauma during their 26.2 mile journey, and they need between one and four weeks to recover from glycogen depletion and the tears between muscle fibres. Adequate recovery is essential if you are to get the most from your running. Consider foregoing running completely after a hard triathlon, substituting the non-weight-bearing sports of cycling and swimming instead.

By ensuring that you take adequate time to recover between training sessions and races, you also ensure that your body has an opportunity to resynthesise glycogen. Without fuel, your muscles' growth and repair will be stymied, and they will be less able to tolerate stress. Furthermore, trying to run with fuel-hungry muscles will result in the recruitment of less energy-deprived muscles, a less economic and fluid running style and eventual injury.

Adequate recovery is, therefore, a

GOAL PACE SESSIONS

Pace min/km	10k goal	800 metre pace	Rest (in seconds)	600 metre pace	Rest (in seconds)
	3,3 33	2' 38"	40		
	3,4 34	2' 43"	41		
	3,5 35	2' 48"	42		
	3,6 36	2' 53"	43		
	3,7 37	2' 58"	44		
	3,8 38	3' 2"	46		
	3,9 39	3' 7"	47		
	4 40	3' 12"	48	2' 24"	48
	4,1 41	3' 17"	49	2' 28"	49
	4,2 42	3' 22"	50	2' 31"	50
	4,3 43	3' 26"	52	2' 35"	52
	4,4 44	3' 31"	53	2' 38"	53
	4,5 45	3' 36"	54	2' 42"	54
	4,6 46	3' 41"	55	2' 46"	55
	4,7 47	3' 46"	56	2' 49"	56
	4,8 48	3' 50"	58	2' 53"	58
	4,9 49	3' 55"	59	2' 56"	59
	5 50	4' 0"	60	3' 0"	60
	5,1 51	4' 5"	61	3' 4"	62
	5,2 52	4' 10"	62	3' 7"	62
	5,3 53	4' 14"	64	3' 11"	64
	5,4 54	4' 19"	65	3' 14"	65
	5,5 55	4' 24"	66	3' 18"	66
	5,6 56	4' 29"	67	3' 22"	67
	5,7 57	4' 34"	68	3' 25"	68
	5,8 58	4' 38"	70	3' 29"	70
	5,9 59	4' 43"	71	3' 32"	71
	6 60	4' 48"	72	3' 36	72

When you do running pace sessions, your 10km goal time should equal the time you take to run 10km in a triathlon, not a 10km on its own. Determine your pace for 600 or 800 metres by finding your triathlon 10km time in this table and then cross-referencing

key element to a successful running programme. So too is a mixed programme of training that incorporates all four kinds of training, and a constant reminder to yourself to make changes to your running programme gradually. Your running schedule has the most

Jonathan Ashby, one of Britain's top triathletes, comes from a swimming background, but has trained himself to be a top notch runner and cyclist too

potential for variety as you can train on:

- Country lanes for your distance work-outs, throwing in a few *fartlek*, or speedplay, sessions.

- Hills for a good strength work out. Run up them more quickly for a VO_2 Max or anaerobic threshold work out; and down them to teach your body to adapt to eccentric muscle contraction – that is when the muscles stretch at the same time as they try to shorten.

You will be familiar with eccentric muscle contractions if you have ever run downhill fast. Two to three days later, your muscles feel sore and tight. Muscle strength falls immediately after a downhill run and recovers ten days later. If you add one downhill session to your weekly running work-outs, you will teach your body to cope with eccentric muscle contractions. But remember, it takes longer to recover from this type of work-out, and if possible, you should refuel – ie eat – immediately after the session.

I can vouch for the effectiveness of eccentric muscle work-outs if they are undertaken with care. Before competing in a 140km, very hilly footrace, which I knew would finish with about a 25km descent, I included weekly downhill running sessions in my training programme. Come race day, I was ninth woman with 25km to go. I knew I could run downhill quickly without feeling too much pain in my quadriceps, so I attacked overtaking

four women, around 20 men and finishing fifth in the women's race. The next day the only soreness I had was on the soles of my feet. Two days later I had packed a rucksack and was heading off into the wilderness for a trek of another 140km.

You can also train on:

- The track – try to find a good quality tartan track, as they tend to be more forgiving on the shins. As with downhill training, the sprint, VO_2 Max and anaerobic threshold training you do on the track is very stressful, so you want as kind a surface as possible, and you must ensure that you allow sufficient time to recover between sessions. Tracks, with their calibrated distances, allow you to run controlled distances and intervals, which are useful in monitoring improvements.

- Stairs or a stair-climbing machine – this might sound odd but a few flights of stairs are a godsend when you are trapped inside during a blizzard. Less stressful are stair-climbing machines, as you don't have the pounding you have on ordinary stairs. Both improve leg strength and cardiovascular fitness.

- A treadmill, when conditions prohibit track work, allows you an opportunity to run intervals, VO_2 Max sessions and anaerobic threshold sessions. You might not be able or willing to run for three hours at a slow pace on a treadmill, but you can usually hold out until exterior conditions change to do your long distance runs.

After you have developed your strength and endurance, your running training should be quality-based. A study conducted on the all-conquering Kenyan runners showed that one reason for their tenacity is that they train at a higher percentage of their capacities. Even their long, slow runs are at a pace that takes them close to or at their anaerobic thresholds. But, remember: most of the Kenyans spent their childhoods building a base of long distance running. Before you try to incorporate 100% quality work-outs in your schedule, build a solid foundation.

Sarah Springman's downhill workout

After a warm-up of at least 15 minutes of easy jogging on the flat, plus some stretching, do at least 10 to 12 x 100 metres of downhill strides. Push your hips forward and allow your legs to turn over quickly while maintaining long powerful strides.

If you are training on a small hill, recover in between strides by jogging very slowly uphill, back to the starting point. If you are on a long continuous descent, jog for twice as long time-wise as your 100 metres effort in between reps. This work-out can be incorporated into a long run.

CHAPTER 8

Transitions

Some say the name triathlon is a misnomer as there are actually four events that make up the sport: swimming, cycling, running and transitions.

Indeed in the early days a great deal of emphasis was placed on transitions spawning the birth of tri-suits, which today are largely forsaken; shoes that could be worn for cycling and running are now recognised as ineffective. Thankfully no one came up with swimming goggles that doubled as sun-shades . . . although that said, someone will probably get on to it right away!

The decline of these products proves the adage of a jack of all trades and master of none. It is not possible to compromise where precision is required. These days many triathletes wear swimsuits with small quick-dry chamois inserts, and a triathlon vest with back pockets, cut long at the back to protect the lumbar region when cycling; cut short at the front to allow

the midriff to stay cool. There is some overlap between sports in terms of clothing but it is still necessary to stop in the transition area and make the change from swimming to cycling mode, and from cycling to running mode.

The aim is still to change over as quickly as possible. To minimise time spent in the transition area make sure that you do the following:

1 Make a mental note of where your bike is racked. Usually you will leave your bike in a pre-determined spot, according to your race number. As you did before you started the swim, look for landmarks that will help you find your spot in the transition area. Make sure that these are large immoveable landmarks: relying on the balloon the organisers have helpfully tied to your bike rack is not a good idea. It might burst and with it will go your plans for a smooth and trouble-free transition.

The transition area: a
mass of frames and
running shoes . . . be
sure to make a note of
exactly where your
bike and kit are before
you start your race

2 Walk the route you plan to take from the swim exit to your bike; from the bike rack to the start of the bike section; from the entry to the transition area back to the bike rack; and finally from where you leave your bike to the start of the run section.

3 Start to remove your wetsuit the minute you stand up in the water. By the time you get to your bike, you should at least have the suit flapping round your hips. Practise taking your wetsuit off against the clock before your first race, so that you are ready for any problems that you might encounter. If the wetsuit is stubborn in places add a dash of petroleum jelly to those areas before you set off on the swim.

4 If the exit from the swim is on sand or gravel, have a small basin of water next to your bike, with a towel laid out ready. When you arrive at the bike rack, step into the basin and then onto the towel to remove any excess sand from your feet, which might otherwise rub and cause discomfort on the bike ride.

5 Lay out a towel in your transition space and put on it the clothing for the bike and run, in the order in which you will don them, eg jersey, helmet, shades and gloves. Place any food you think you will need for the bike ride next to your jersey, putting it into pockets after you have your jersey on, unless you can be absolutely sure that it won't all tip out as you pull the jersey over

Left: you will often be required to wheel your bike in and out of the transition area, as this athlete is doing in the 1992 Bath Triathlon. This is a safety measure and failure to comply with it will result in penalties for you and could lead to an accident or injury

Right: one trick of the trade is to dress on the run. You'll note that this triathlete is wearing his race number on an elastic band around his waist. The number is worn on his back during the bike ride and, after he's pulled on his singlet, it will be displayed on his front for the run

your head. If you use PowerBars, you can simply fold them over your bike's top tube. This works even better if you have a fat-tubed bike such as a Cannondale.

6 Try leaving your bike shoes fixed to your clipless pedals. This way, you can wheel your bike out of the transition area and slip your feet into the pedals while you are riding. Be sure you are adept at this before trying it in a race situation – you might be faster sitting down in the transition area to put on your shoes than wobbling about on your bike trying to do it.

As you approach the transition area after the bike ride, extract your feet from your shoes as you are moving and pedal the last 200 metres of the bike course with your feet

on top of the shoes. When you dismount leave the shoes in the pedals. To knock another couple of seconds off your transitions practise smooth cyclo-cross dismounts.

7 Some triathletes use lace-locks for their running and cycling shoes. These save a couple of seconds but they are not a prerequisite to success.

8 Always keep an extra bottle of water in your personal transition area, and take a sip from it as you enter and leave the transition area. If you have just completed a swim in salty water, you might want to keep some tinned peaches near your bike, to take away any biliousness caused by sea-water.

The transition area is
the site of much
activity – some would
say mayhem – during
a triathlon

Besides the clothing and equipment
aspect, the change from one sport to
another requires a period of adjustment
for your body. These adjustments start
before you enter the transition area.

1 In swimming, you will notice the change
when you stand up to leave the water. You
may feel dizzy, but this should pass. It is a
result of transferring quickly from an
horizontal to a vertical position, the blood
which has been helping your arm muscles to
do the work during the swim being
reallocated to other parts of the body. This
phenomenon could be more pronounced in
cold water and is essentially unavoidable,
but it is something you grow accustomed to
as you become a more experienced

Triathlete. Try to stand up slowly after the
swim, uncurling from your horizontal
position, and pulling into a full, upright
position gently. If you feel excessively dizzy,
walk out of the water, don't run. Once on
dry land, stop until the sensation passes.

2 On the bike to run transition, remember
that you will be asking your agonist and
antagonist muscles to swop tasks, ie the
quadriceps that were contracting on the bike
ride will be lengthening during the run. You
might feel as if someone is stabbing you in
the legs on your first attempt at this transition.
Even if you normally run like a gazelle,
you will probably not feel as fluid as you
usually do. The discomfort of the bike-to-
run transition is an unavoidable fact in
triathlon, but it gets easier with time.

To help yourself along, try:

- Changing into an easy gear in the closing stages of the bike and spinning your pedal at high revs.

- Standing on the pedals and stretching out your back and legs.

- Once in the transition area, sit down to put on your shoes. This will allow you to recover slightly.

- Do one or two hamstring and lower back stretches before setting off on the run. You can do these in one flowing movement as you stand up, and they will only add a matter of seconds to your transition. Cross one leg in front of the other as you stand up, front leg bent, back leg straight. Unbend from the waist, lengthening along the spine as you do so, and lace up one shoe. Change legs and do the other.

As with all of triathlon's components, your ideal transition can only be achieved by you, after trial and error. The ideal is one which allows you sufficient time to transfer mentally and physically from one sport to another, without wasting precious seconds, and without breaking the transition area rules. The most important of these are:

- Rack your bike neatly and carefully in the slot allocated to you. In some larger triathlons, there will be helpers on hand to do this for you, but generally speaking that is a luxury.

- Enter and leave the transition area by the means of locomotion permitted by the race organiser. You may not be allowed to ride your bike in the transition area, and will have to wheel it out onto the race course.

- Don't remove your helmet or unfasten it until you're off the bike.

Triathlons can be won or lost in the transition area, but it is not always the fastest out of the transition area who will be the first across the line. Transitions are a time to think about your comfort during the bike ride, a chance to unwind before going into the run. Some triathletes will be able to leap off the bike or out of the water, and fly straight into the next discipline. Others will not, and if they try to cut corners in the transition area, they will only pay during the bike or run sections.

CHAPTER 9

Stretching

Stretching should be as indispensable a part of your triathlon training programme as swimming, cycling and running. Done properly, it can protect you from injury and can be useful in helping you to relax, important in the hectic schedule of a triathlete. Improper stretching, on the other hand, can do just the opposite.

Unfortunately, most people don't stretch correctly. They jerk their muscles and joints into a stretched position. They bend from the waist, get their head as close to their knees as they can – and then bounce. They think they are doing themselves good, but in fact, they are deriving very little benefit from their frantic activity. By bouncing or otherwise overstretching, you activate something called the stretch reflex. A signal is sent to your brain to say that your muscles are being stretched too far, and the brain responds by sending back a signal to the muscles to tell them to contract. So,

ironically, the muscle you thought you were stretching is, in fact, contracting.

Overstretching also leads to tiny tears in the muscles, which can lead to a build-up of scar tissue, which will eventually equate to a loss of elasticity.

Correct stretching should be progressive and painless. Start with an easy stretch, which is characterised by a feeling of mild tension. Hold this for 20 to 30 seconds, and note how the feeling of tension subsides. If it doesn't, ease off the stretch a bit.

After this 20 to 30 second phase of easy stretching, during which you **do not** bounce, you are ready to move onto the next phase: developmental stretching. Extend slightly further into your stretch, until the tension increases, but only slightly. Hold for 20 to 30 seconds. And remember, do not bounce.

Also remember to breathe while you stretch. If you are unable to breathe, then you aren't relaxed and your

Shoulder flexibility is an important ingredient in successful swimming. In addition to following a regular stretching programme keep a few quick stretches in your repertoire to help you to loosen up before a race

stretch is probably not doing you much good.

Breathe from your abdomen. Practise your breathing by lying on your back on the floor, knees bent and soles of your feet flat on the ground. Place your hands on either side of your stomach. Close your eyes, relax, and inhale, pushing your stomach out as you do so. On the exhalation, push your stomach inward. Try to touch your spinal cord with the wall of your stomach as you do so. Exaggerate the

stomach movements during this exercise and take note of how they feel. Think of your abdominal muscles as a bellows for your lungs. By combining relaxed, deep, abdominal breathing with correctly executed stretching, you will, at worst, enrich your life as a triathlete and, at best, improve your performance – which in turn enriches your life. You can't lose, really.

A well-planned stretching programme should be incorporated into your warm-up and cool-down sessions, thereby helping you to avoid injury and also to relieve muscle soreness. Stretching can also be practised independently from any other exercise, in order to improve or maintain flexibility, and to help you to relax.

The following are stretching exercises specific to triathlon's sports and can be practised at any time of day. When you try them, remember to:

- start with an easy stretch

- progress to a developmental stretch

- never stop breathing

- relax your body and mind

- never, ever bounce.

Ten gentle stretches for triathletes

1 Sit on the ground, legs stretched out in front of you. Lean back and rest on your elbows, forearms parallel to your hips. Bend your knees and slide your bottom forward on the ground, keeping your forearms and elbows still. You should feel a stretch in the shoulders. Hold for 20 to 30 seconds at easy stretch; then slide your bottom a bit further along the ground and hold for another 20 to 30 seconds. Rest and repeat. *Deltoid, shoulder muscles*

2 Lie on your back on the ground. Bend your knees and bring the soles of your feet together so that you form a diamond with your legs. With your hands resting gently on your stomach, and remembering to breathe, push your knees down toward the ground. Easy stretch, hold 30 seconds, then push a little further and hold for 30 seconds. Relax. *Adductor muscles, quadriceps, hip joint*

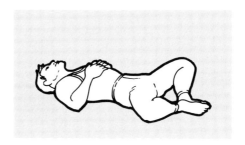

3 Sit up and extend your legs in front of you. Keeping your back straight, bend your right leg at the knee and place your right foot on the left side of your left leg. Now, turn to the right from the torso, and place your left elbow on the outside of your right knee. Place your right hand behind you, and turn as far as you can from the torso, to look behind and upwards. Hold for 20 seconds, then turn a fraction more. Relax and repeat on other side.
Lower back, abductor muscles

4 Still sitting, stretch both legs out in front of you. Dropping forward from the waist, run your hands as far as they will go along the outside of your legs. Drop your head toward your knees, but don't force. Grab your legs with your hands, and gently pull yourself down. Hold at easy stretch then drop a fraction further. Feel the stretch down your spine. Repeat two to four times.
Lower back and hamstring

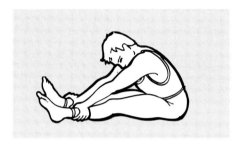

5 Stand up, feet shoulder-width apart. Turn the left foot so that it is facing forward and

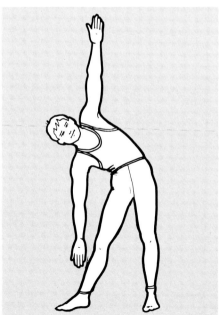

in line with your shoulder. The right foot facing outwards, slide it 12 – 18 inches to the right. While breathing in raise both arms out to shoulder level, palms facing forward. Without moving your feet, and keeping your hips facing forward, bend from the waist to the right while exhaling, until your arms are as vertical as you can comfortably manage. Hold, inhale and exhale deeply once, dropping slightly further to the right on exhalation. Then return to starting position. Repeat other side.
Lower back, waist and hips

6 In a standing position, clasp your hands behind your back. Pull up with one hand on the other. Repeat other side. (If you are unable to clasp your hands behind your back, hold a towel between the two and pull on the towel.)
Shoulders

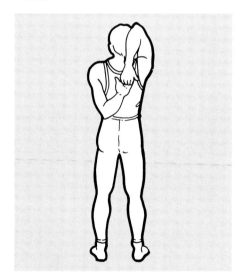

7 In a standing position, place your hands against a wall and extend one leg behind you. The other leg should be bent at the knee and closer to the wall. Gently push the

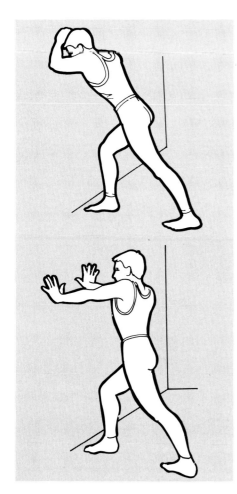

8 Still standing, grasp your right foot with your left hand behind your buttocks. Hold for 20 seconds. Change legs.
Quadriceps

9 Kneel on the ground, buttocks resting on your heels. Place your hands behind you and rock back easily so that your weight is taken by your hands and your knees are raised off the ground. Hold (it isn't easy).
Ankles and quadriceps

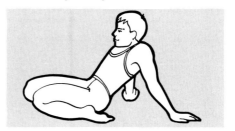

heel of the extended leg toward the ground. Hold for 30 seconds, then move back leg in bend knee to 'sit down'. Change legs.
Calves, Achilles tendon

10 Lie down on the ground, hands extended above your head, legs stretched out. Stretch along the entire length of your body. Enjoy it.

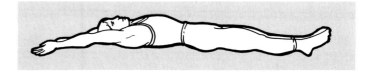

CHAPTER 10

Training for strength

With the time constraints that beset triathletes, and the need to train the muscles used in three different sports, it should be clear to you that you'll need to give the formulation of an efficient strength training schedule a bit of thought. Take heart: a good strength training session can take as little as half an hour, and you don't even need to go to a gym.

It should be pointed out that weight training is not an ideal addition to everyone's programme. If you are a heavily muscled man, then you might be wise to forego the weight training. On the other hand, many women can reap great benefits from it. The fastest woman's time will always be slower than the fastest man's partly because of their inferior muscle bulk. But, to redress the balance somewhat, a trained muscle in a woman is said to be as strong as a trained muscle in her male counterpart.

Training with weights will enhance your ability to swim, bike and run, but it cannot replace specific training for each sport. As you plan your strength training programme, consider the following:

1 Your weight training year should be divided, as is the rest of your training year, into training periods.

2 You should try to set up a programme which allows you to train all the muscles used in triathlon, which takes your joints through a full range of motion, and which then allows adequate time to recover.

3 Rather than follow a traditional, static gym workout, try to keep your weight training active, so that you are training aerobically as well as anaerobically. For example do jumping jacks between sets, or run around your gym's indoor track, if there is one.

4 Try to work antagonistic muscles in one group of exercises. For example, if you

When you design a weight training programme remember that you are not aiming to beef up too much. All that muscle bulk will slow you down

work the biceps in your arms for ten reps, work the triceps next, then back to the biceps. Natural movements always work your biceps and triceps together.

5 Always start with light weights and build up gradually. This applies to a session or to strength training in general

6 Always, always warm up.

Getting started

Start with minimum repetitions and sets with light weights. To determine the maximum weight you should use in a given exercise, start with no weight on the bar or stack of the machine. Do ten repetitions. Then, after a rest, add the minimum additional weight that the bar or machine permits. Do another ten reps. Rest. Continue until you find a weight at which you cannot comfortably complete ten reps. Drop down one level of intensity from there: this is the maximum intensity to which you should work.

- A rep is one full movement of a given exercise.

- A set is any number of groups of reps, interrupted by a rest interval.

- Always start any weights exercise at low intensity. If you intend to do four high intensity sets, build up to your maximum.

- Weights should be increased gradually. If, for example, you start a set with 10kg on a barbell, you may increase to 15kgs in the second set and 20kgs in the third. Never jump drastically in terms of weight.

- Don't sacrifice good form for high weights. You won't be exercising efficiently, and you will be increasing your risk of injury.

- Breathe! Inhale during the recovery phase; exhale on exertion.

Following the basic year's training breakdown, your 12-month weight training schedule should look something like this:

Rest and build 1: the first part of the Rest and Build Phase, which falls immediately after the close of your triathlon season, gives you a chance to recuperate mentally and physically from triathlon. If you want to train with weights, do so, but keep the sessions very, very easy. Work out with light weights to keep yourself ticking over, or do the exercises without weights described below.

Rest and build 2: probably the most important phase in your strength training programme. You can draw parallels between the strength training you are doing during this phase of your training year and the long, slow distance training in swimming, cycling and running. Both are laying down foundations on which you will build in the coming months.

Start by training with weights three times a week if possible, doing 50% of the exercises listed below with three to five sets per exercise. Increase reps first, then gradually increase weights. By the end of the period, you should see a ten percent increase in both.

Rest and build 3: increase the building phase. Alternate three- and four-day weeks in the gym, ie work out with weights every other day. If your aim is to increase your strength, then increase maximum weight on each set gradually throughout the month, judging the permissible increase by the way you feel during and after a work-out. If your muscles are very sore or if you are unduly tired, do not increase weights. Keep reps as in Rest and build 2. If you are already muscular, then concentrate on increasing reps, not intensity.

Vary your sessions: if you want to concentrate on your legs in one session, do all the leg exercises listed below, plus one arm and one upper body exercise. Try to do 50% of the exercises and three to five sets of each per session.

Pre-season: you should spend most of your time doing anaerobic threshold work. The time devoted to weight training should therefore be reduced slightly. Work out two times a week as outlined above. Do at least 75% of the exercises listed below, and do between three to four sets of each. Increase reps in the first month and hold in the second month. In the second month, increase weight, or intensity, by ten percent over the entire month. In the third month, maintain the levels for both reps and intensity.

Pre-competition: six weeks to go before the event. Work out two times a week, but with decreased intensity and increased reps.

Competition: two weeks to go. Train two times a week if desired. Decrease weights to your pre-season level. Increase reps to maximum. Do not weight train for two to four days before the event.

During the competitive season, you may completely forego weight training if you wish. The time devoted to weight training is time that you might need to recover from races. Gauge your needs and organise your programme accordingly.

Immediate post-competiton (during the race season): for one week, reduce visits to the gym, as well as the intensity of your sessions – ie use weights as at the beginning of your pre-competition phase. Do a medium number of reps per exercise. Then restart with pre-competition phase week two, visiting the gym two to three times a week and build up to your next big race.

At the end of the racing season treat yourself to a rest before you start rebuilding for the next season.

As your body becomes used to the strain of training, it gets better at recuperating, assuming you give it adequate time to do so. If in the beginning you needed two days between sessions to recover, you might find that you only need one as your strength increases. One good way to tell if you need a bit of extra recovery time is the soreness in your muscles. A little tenderness is not a bad thing, but tight, aching muscles are a · message from your body telling you to relax.

Concentrate on isotonic exercises, which are the most common in weight training. The entire muscle is worked and strengthened by lengthening and shortening it during exercise. Machines (Nautilus or Universal, for example) and barbells and dumb-bells are commonly used in isotonic exercises.

The Session

Remember to warm-up first. A good warm-up should consist of a stretching routine and some aerobic work, so that you are in a light sweat when you begin your weights sessions. If you train in a gym, try ten minutes on the treadmill or stair climbing machine after your stretching exercises and before weight training.

The exercises

Bench press Lying face-up on a bench, grab barbell, thumbs under the bar, hands far enough apart (probably about 2 feet/60 cm) so that when the bar is resting on your chest, your upper arms are parallel to the floor and your forearms are vertical. Press the weight up from your chest until your arms are fully extended. Then lower the weight down toward your chest. Touch the bar lightly to your chest and then press upwards again. Keep your elbows under the bar – don't bring them in towards

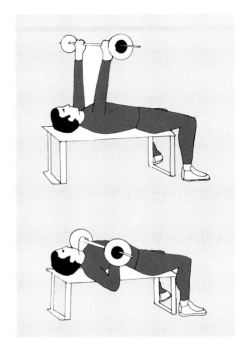

your body. *Works upper pectorals, triceps and deltoids.*

Pec-Deck Adjust the level of the seat of a pec-deck machine (in most gyms) so that your elbows are parallel to the floor when they touch the pads. Your forearms should be relaxed and resting vertically on the pads.

Muscles	Exercise	Reps	Sets
Quadriceps	Leg Extensions	10 – 20	2 – 5
Hamstrings	Leg Curls	10 – 20	2 – 5
Thighs/hips	Squats	10 – 20	2 – 5
Adductors	Adductor machine	10 – 20	2 – 5
Calves	Standing calf raise	10 – 20	2 – 5
Abdominals	Partial sit-ups	10 – 30	1 – 5
	Oblique sit-ups	10 – 30	1 – 5
with			
Lower Back	Good mornings	10 – 30	1 – 4
or Hyperextension			
Lats (upper back)	Pull downs	10 – 20	2 – 4
Lower lats	Close grip pull down	10 – 20	2 – 4
Biceps	Bicep curls	10 – 20	2 – 4
Triceps	Tricep pull-downs	10 – 20	2 – 4
Shoulders	Military press	10 – 15	2 – 4
	Upright rowing	10 – 20	2 – 4
Chest	Bench press	10 – 15	2 – 4
	Incline flies	10 – 15	2 – 4
	Pec Deck	10 – 25	2 – 4

Push the pads of the pec-deck together, concentrating on generating the push from your pectoral, or chest muscles. Control the pads as you return to the starting postion. Works chest muscles.

Incline flies Lie face-up, feet on the ground, on a bench inclined at 30 – 40 degrees. Keeping elbows slightly bent throughout, lower a pair of dumb-bells slowly from a starting position with your arms extended above your chest to a point where they are parallel to the floor. Keep weights under control throughout the exercise. Don't arch your back. *Works upper chest.*

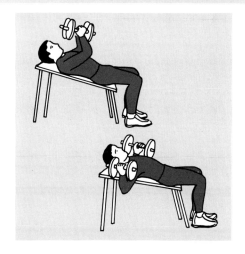

Good mornings Stand with feet shoulder width apart, a light barbell across your shoulders. NOTE: Start with the bar only, as this exercise stresses an historically weak part of the body. Keep your back straight as you bend forward from the waist. Return to start position. Works lower back. And I don't know why they're called good mornings.

Hyperextensions These are usually performed on a machine specially designed for the purpose. If one is not to hand, lie on a bench and get a friend to hold your ankles firmly. With your upper body bending freely below the machine or bench, raise and lower yourself until your upper body is parallel with the floor. *Works lower back.*

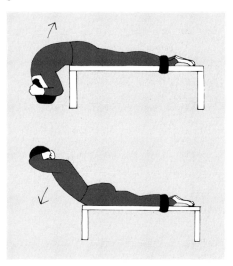

Lat pull downs Using a lat machine, take a wide grip on the overhead bar. Pull it down, keeping your back straight, until the bar touches the top of your back. Return under to control to start position.

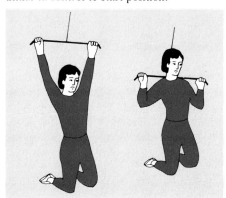

Close-grip pull down Either using the same wide bar on the lat machine but gripping it *with your hands close together*, or changing for a bar that allows a narrow grip, pull the bar down to the front of the chest. Return the arms to a straight position and repeat.

Military press It is preferable to use a machine for this, as it minimises the risk of straining the lower back. Sit with your back straight. Raise and lower the machine's bar, with your hands slightly wider than shoulder width apart. At its lowest level, the bar should be just above your shoulders; at

its highest level, your arms should be straight. Continue the up and down arm motion with one fluid action. *Works back, deltoids and triceps.*

Upright rowing Stand holding a barbell, hands four to six inches apart in front of your thighs, arms straight. Raise your hands as high as you can towards your chin, bending your arms at the elbows keeping the bar close to your chest. Point the elbows outwards, and don't lean backwards. *Works deltoids and biceps.*

Squats Using either a barbell (make sure someone is spotting you) or a squat machine, stand with your feet about shoulder width apart, bar resting across your shoulders. Keeping your heels on the floor and your back straight, slowly lower yourself into a squat position. Return to starting position, always controlling the weight. *Works thighs and hips.*

Leg curl Lie on your stomach on the bench of a leg-curl machine. Place your heels under the lift-pad. Raise the machine's weight by curling your legs upwards until they are at about an 80-90 degree bend. Release slowly. *Works hamstrings.*

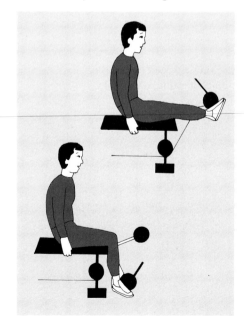

Leg extension Sitting upright, place the front of your ankles under the lift pad of a leg-extension machine. With your back straight and holding the grips at the side of the machine, extend your legs in a controlled fashion from the knee, lifting the weight at the back of the machine. Lower down to the starting position. *Works quadriceps.*

Calf raise Stand with the balls of your feet on the pad of a calf-raise machine. Two pads should rest comfortably on your shoulders. Raise up onto your toes, then return to the start position. *Works calf muscles and Achilles.*

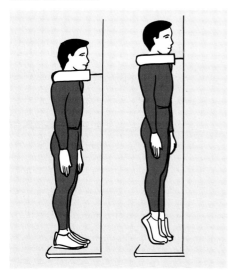

Triceps pull down Keeping your elbows at your sides, pull the bar of a lat machine or triceps machine downwards from mid-chest until your arms are straight.

Biceps curl Hold a barbell with your hands slightly wider than shoulder width apart. Keep your elbows close to your body and curl the weight up towards your chin. Return to start position.

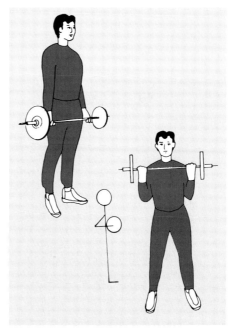

Through weight training you are:

- increasing the strength of your muscles, ie the force they can exert

- teaching your fast-twitch muscles to work more effectively

- helping your muscles to remain at maximum exertion for a longer period of time

There are isotonic training sessions you can do without having access to a gym. Try:

Squats Without using a weight, execute the same motion as described before, but increase the number of number repetitions working up to 100.

Sissy squats Holding a wall or bench for support, raise up onto your toes and lean back very slightly. Then, still on your toes and your back straight, sink slowly and with control into a shallow squat. Return to start position and repeat. This is harder than you think, so start with ten and work up to 30 continuous sissy squats. *Works lower quadriceps.*

Lunges Starting from an upright position, feet together, step forward with one leg, extending the other straight behind you. The heel of the front leg should be flat on the ground, and you should bend the knee so that you lunge into as deep a position as you can. Then return to the start position, by moving the bent leg, not the extended, rear leg. One lunge per leg equals one rep. Do 10 continuous reps and work up to 30. *Works gluteals and quadriceps.*

Triceps press-ups Sit on the floor, with a low bench behind you. You should be facing away from the bench, legs *extended* in front of you. Place the palms of your hands on the bench. Raise and lower your body by straightening and bending your arms at the elbow. Do three to five sets of 10 to 20 repetitions.

Press-ups Turn and face the bench. With your arms slightly wider than shoulder width apart, place your hands on the bench and raise and lower your body by straightening and bending your arms. Chest, shoulders and biceps. Do three to five sets of 10 to 20 repetitions.

You might want to incorporate these into a running session. If you schedule them to fall after about 15 minutes of running, they'll help to warm you up and will break up a long run session.

Partial sit-ups Lie on the floor with your knees raised. Place your hands behind your head, and keep your elbows pointing outward. Without pulling up on your head with your arms, raise up from the shoulders, then lower back to the ground. *Works abdominals.*

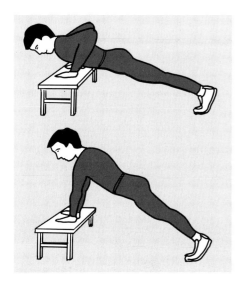

Oblique sit-ups As above, but cross one leg over the other, resting the right foot on the left knee. As you raise yourself from the shoulders, twist from the waist and touch your right elbow to the left knee. Repeat for at least ten reps on one side, then change sides and complete an equal number of reps, to give you one set. *Works abdominals, and obliques.*

CHAPTER 11

Cross-training

In the early days of triathlon, it was a unique concept that a runner should cycle or that a swimmer should run. Now, athletes who take up triathlon accept that they are going to be training at swimming, cycling and running. The concept once referred to as cross-training is now known, quite simply, as triathlon training.

Cross-training pre-dates the relatively young sport of triathlon. Many athletes take up another sport when injury prevents them from practising their primary activity. This is a variety of cross-training, and it is a good reason for training at more than one sport. By dividing your training demands between all of your muscle groups, the risk of injury is reduced.

Another form of cross-training is practising one sport in summer and a different one in winter: the cyclist who speed skates or the moto-cross rider who skis, for instance. Both are deriving benefits from their secondary sport which they transfer to their primary one. Speed skating, for instance, helps to develop strength and endurance, while skiing and moto-cross are mutually beneficial sports because they help to develop lightning quick motor reactions. Even if there are no immediately obvious physical benefits to cross-training, there could be very helpful motor benefits, for example enhanced reaction times.

The difference in triathlon is that **all** the component sports are primary sports. By shifting the training emphasis from one sport, and therefore one muscle group, to another, you can train for longer than you would if you were training at just one sport. Covering the 140.6 miles of the Hawaii Ironman is arguably easier than completing the 72 mile Grande Traversée of Reunion Island, a non-stop run. In the Ironman, the effort is divided between your swimming, cycling and running muscles. In the

A lean physique will be a great help to you on the run. Ideally a triathlete should aim for a balance of leanness and muscle to help him or her excel at all three component sports

Grande Traversée, it's legs, legs, legs.

Besides enhancing your aerobic fitness, cross-training also develops your muscles in the right proportions to compete at triathlon. In cycling, your quadriceps muscles contract and initiate movement, ie to extend the leg from the hip. They act as agonists. The hamstrings perform what is known as an antagonistic function: they contract and shorten to pull up on the pedal. In running, the reverse takes place. The opposite agonistic-antagonistic actions of running and cycling explain why the transition between the two sports in a triathlon can be so difficult. If you only rode a bike or ran, your muscles would be unused to the action of the other sport. By cross-training, you accustom your muscles to the strain they will be subjected to in the next event.

For those new to triathlon, there are ways of training for more than one sport without overdoing it:

1 Don't train at all of triathlon's sports everyday. To do so would only result in overtraining.

2 The phenomenon known as back-to-back training – ie cycling immediately after swimming or running immediately after cycling – is useful if you want to acquaint yourself with the sensations of triathlon, but you do not have to make back-to-back

Mountain biking not only builds muscle strength but also improves your bike handling skills and provides excellent aerobic exercise. A dirt trail amidst greenery makes a nice change to the tarmac most triathletes are used to

training a regular part of your training. Excessive use of this method will only tire you emotionally and physically and raise your chances of injury.

3 Training for 45 minutes in the swimming pool will not produce the same effects as training for 45 minutes on the running track. Of triathlon's sports, swimming is the least demanding physiologically, but the most demanding technically.

Frank Shorter, a former Olympic marathon champion who turned to duathlon (run and bike) when injury stopped him running, calculated that to get the equivalent training effect of a good six to seven mile run, he had to ride for 45 to minutes to an hour at a steady pulse rate of 140 beats per minute. When determining your own training effect equivalents, bear in mind the distance of each work-out, whether your effort is continuous or broken into several separate repeats, and how long you rest between repeats. By knowing your training equivalents, you will be in a position to substitute an equivalent indoor cycling session if injury or weather conditions prevent you from running. Don't be fooled into thinking that one sport can entirely replace the other.

4 Recovery times will be different for the three sports. Running is the most stressful of triathlon's component sports and therefore requires the longest recovery time.

5 When you take up cross- or triathlon training, allow yourself a buffer period to make the biomechanical transition from one sport to another. You should need about two weeks to feel comfortable with a new sport, and six weeks for your body to adapt physiologically to it.

Alternative training

Triathlon is a summer sport, and during the high season, you will be up to your neck in training and racing. Despite having your attention divided between three different sports, you might sometimes find yourself bored with the same old routine.

There are also times when you may have a forced lay-off from triathlon, through injury.

Never fear: during the season, and more readily during the off-season, you can replace your normal swim, bike and run sessions with alternative work-outs.

Try going for an off-road mountain bike ride instead of doing a hill run or a bike session, for instance. Mountain biking is more stressful than road riding; it requires better bike handling skills; and a good session requires less time than a road bike session. In addition, a mountain bike ride that includes a lot of climbing is helpful in building your quadriceps muscles and provides an excellent cardiovascular work-out.

Rollerblading or in-line skating, is a non-weight-bearing aerobic exercise. Use it in place of cycling. If you have a running injury, rollerblading could help to keep you in good aerobic shape, while not stressing your joints the way running does.

Rowing, canoeing, kayaking are all non-weight bearing and all tax the cardiovascular system. Rowing requires more leg work than you probably imagine, and canoeing gives your abdominal muscles an unexpected workout. All three work the upper body.

Snow and ice don't necessarily mean that you have to stop training. A short break is good, both mentally and physically. But winter is a great time for a change of sport: try ice-biking with studded fat tyres, or downhill, or cross-country skiing

During the winter, if snow on the ground makes running and cycling impossible or even dangerous, try:

Snowshoeing The sport where you run around with things resembling tennis rackets on your feet. Snowshoes allow you to run or walk on the snow, without sinking into it. Try snowing to the top of a hill and back – you'll be convinced that it is a good winter alternative to running.

Mountain biking Yes, you can do it in winter too. You need to get specially studded tyres, and it is even harder than it is during the summer. But it keeps your cycling muscles in trim.

Cross-country skiing Said to be the best sport going for promoting aerobic fitness. Cross-country skiing also works the muscles you need for running and cycling – more the latter. If you are new to cross-country skiing, take a few

lessons and learn how to climb with skis, and how to skate.

Downhill skiing builds your thigh muscles and sharpens your reaction times.

As if to prove the point that triathlon doesn't stop when the snow is on the ground, there are winter multi-sport events, which are often won by the swim, bike and run summer specialists. And more and more triathlons incorporating mountain bike sections are being organised in the summer months.

At the very least, these alternative events and sports add more variety to your programme. But remember, to excel at a given sport, you have to devote a lot of time to perfecting your specific skills at that sport. So as soon as you can put the skis back in the garage and get the bike out of mothballs, do.

Jan Ripple of the United States has a very muscular build for a triathlete, but that hasn't stopped her from scoring some excellent results in her career. In 1989 she was runner up to Erin Baker in the World Championships, and she has also finished in the top three in the Ironman

Massage is a useful addition to a triathlete's regular regime. A post-race massage is a good way to unwind and prevent muscle stiffness

Most triathlon injuries are due to overuse. Forcing yourself through training when you first notice the onset of an injury will only exacerbate the problem

CHAPTER 12

Injuries
By Dr Domhnall MacAuley

Triathlon is a relatively safe sport offering balanced whole body exercise with little of the trauma associated with many other sports. Most of the injuries that do occur are usually due to overuse, but even overuse injury is uncommon in the athlete who cross-trains.

While cardiovascular fitness is common to all endurance sports, training is so specific that the physiological benefits from cycling, swimming or running are not fully transferable. The best form of training for a sport is that sport, and there is no substitute for sustained intensive and extensive training in each discipline. Unfortunately the athlete runs the risk of three sets of overuse injuries as well as the threat of overtraining. You should always be aware of the fine line between load and overload, training and overtraining.

Generally speaking, running injuries are typically associated with high mileage, pavement pounding; cycling has a smooth non-jarring action but has its own specific injuries; while swimming carries the threat of shoulder problems and ear trouble. Here they are in detail:

Swimming

In theory, swimming is a safe aerobic sport. That is unless you have fallen foul of swimmer's ear, breast-stroker's knee or crawler's shoulder!

Swimmer's ear is the itchy inflammation of the delicate skin lining the ear canal and is often accompanied by bacterial infection, irritation and a discharge. It is most common in those who spend a lot of time in the water – fresh water in particular. When the sensitive skin lining the ear canal becomes wet and macerated due to constant immersion it loses its normal oily protective coating. It should be dried gently with a clean towel as rough cleansing can cause skin breakdown leading to infection. The ear canal may become acutely inflamed and so painful that even a gentle tug on the ear lobe may be agony. Inflammation is usually treated with combined anti-inflammatory/antibiotic ear drops but severe infection may require oral antibiotics. Ear plugs help prevent water entering the ear canal and the newer silicone plugs offer better protection.

Breast-stroker's knee is a nagging pain on the inside of the knee. The constant repetitive kick in the breast-stroke stretches ligaments which run across the inside of the knee joint, causing a chronic medial ligament strain. Treatment is to use ice initially, and to visit a physiotherapist who may use ultrasound to ease the condition. It is also worth seeking the advice of a coach who may suggest modifications to your stroke action.

Crawler's shoulder is a chronic overuse injury of the shoulder muscles. As the swimmer draws the arm up, overhead, the group of muscles known as the rotator cuff are compressed under the arch of bone and ligaments at the top of the shoulder, causing pain and inflammation. Treatment is by altering the stroke. Severe cases may require an injection of an anti-inflammatory in the tender points.

Painful red eyes are often due to conjunctivitis from chemical irritation as a result of constant exposure to chlorine and other preparations used to keep pools clean. The key to prevention is in protecting the eyes by wearing goggles. The condition may be helped by cleansing with a proprietary eyewash. Sore red eyes are not usually due to an infection, but if an infection develops it requires treatment with antibiotics.

Running

Triathletes usually include distance and interval training in their running programme. Injuries occur when you build up your training load too high, too soon, or with a change in training surface. To avoid injury, train sensibly with a gradual build up of mileage and intensity. A good rule of thumb is never increase the training load or intensity by more than 10% per week, and for some even this may be too steep.

Use good quality well-cushioned shoes that are specifically designed for running. As triathletes are often well-muscled individuals, heavier than most distance runners, the top of the range 8oz-racer may not be for you; you may need extra support and cushioning.

The running surface is important too: try to run on grass wherever possible, asphalt is less stressful than concrete, and sand can be a high impact surface particularly close to the water's edge where it is packed.

Although cycling and running use similar muscles (the quadriceps at the front of the thigh, hamstrings at the back and the soleus and gastrocnemeus, which make up the

Mike Pigg, one of the
second generation of
triathletes, runs to
victory in the 1990
Portsmouth Triathlon

calf) the type of muscle contraction is quite different. Cycling is a non-weight bearing sport with a constant, smooth action. In contrast, with each running step the heel strikes the ground at a force of up to 10 times the body's weight. With each stride the muscle contracts but is sharply stretched at the same time. The impact of each stride not only jars the bones, but also stretches the soft tissues, muscles and tendons which causes micro-trauma (muscle damage at cellular level).

Shin Splints is the catch-all name for pain at the front of the lower leg, most commonly caused by stress fracture. Unused to impact stress, the bones may develop tiny fractures – similar to metal fatigue in aircraft – usually caused by too much, too soon, too fast, with shoes that are too old. The first warning of it is pain that occurs in training becoming more severe through the run. As the condition progresses pain may also occur at rest or at night.

The treatment is rest, but prevention is better than cure, and stress fractures may be prevented by taking care over your training programme. Increase running mileage gradually; try to train on a forgiving surface such as grass; and wear shoes with good shock absorbency. Some athletes run with an abnormal gait and may benefit from a special insole called an orthotic, which helps to correct the gait, reducing stress on the lower leg. Other causes of shin splints include periostitis – an inflammation of the lining of the bone – and compartment syndrome, where the exercising muscle is restricted by surrounding tissue. These require specialist advice and treatment.

Achilles tendinitis often affects endurance athletes through the constant repetitive stretch and stress on muscles and tendons. The Achilles tendon joins the muscles of the lower calf, the gastrocnemeus and soleus, to the heel bone, the calcaneus. The symptoms of inflammation or tenderness are often aggravated by abnormalities in gait or inappropriate shoes.

In the early stages of this condition there is stiffness in the morning which eases through the day, but as the condition progresses the pain increases with persistent stiffness throughout the day. Running may cause pain, but it is only usually present at the start of exercise, easing during the run, and returning with increased stiffness after a few hours' rest. Severe tendinitis causes painful swelling of the tendon which is tender to touch and painful during exercise.

Achilles tendinitis is essentially an overuse injury, although footwear can sometimes be the culprit, especially if the shoes have a heel tab at the back. While the tab looks good and helps to provide a snug fit, it may impinge on the tendon when running: the back of the shoe is forced into the tendon at take off on every stride. A similar movement can occur in cycling at the bottom of each pedal revolution if you pedal with your toes pointing down.

The treatment is surgery – to the shoe. Cut a semi-circle at the back, removing the entire heel tab, or cut two slits on either side of the heel tab so that it flops loosely at the back of the shoe. This should ensure that no part of the shoe restricts the movement of the Achilles tendon.

Remember to check your other shoes if you are recovering from this condition. It may help to take the stretch off the tendon by wearing a heel raise; specially moulded shoe-inserts are available from most sports shops. Physiotherapy is also beneficial: some of the treatments available include ultrasound, laser, friction massage and stretching exercises. Non-steroidal anti-inflammatory drugs (NSAIDs) help to reduce pain and swelling in soft tissue but have side-effects and should be used under medical supervision. NSAIDs are also available as topical gels and these offer safe, effective treatment. Injections should be avoided around the Achilles tendon: they give only short-term relief, may cause weakening, and may lead to tendon rupture. Rupture will mean a minimum of eight weeks in plaster, with or without surgery – that's an entire season.

Cycling

Cycling is the least hazardous of triathlon's three sports, but it does carry the risk of one common menace:

Knee injuries are almost an occupational hazard for those in cycle training, and can be the result of pedalling at 100rpm for four to five hours or of improper bike set up. Pain behind the kneecap is a common symptom. Normally the kneecap slides smoothly up and down a groove on the thigh bone and stays in the groove because of equal pull on either side of the kneecap. When the load on the knee is too great, forcing it against the groove, or if the pull is not equal, drawing it out of the groove, pain results. These are known as loading or tracking problems.

The secret of reducing the excess load is in finding the right pedalling cadence: cycling in a lower gear at a higher pedal rate ensures that while the bike travels at the same speed there is less pressure on the kneecap at each pedal stroke. With a tracking problem, the muscle tends to draw the kneecap out of the groove causing friction on the reverse side of the kneecap. Prevention of pain depends not only on reducing loading on the knee but also in preventing alignment problems, and for this you will probably need the help of a coach.

Knee pain is often associated with a sudden jump in mileage at the beginning of a season or following a period off the bike due to illness or holidays. There is a temptation to compensate by increasing the mileage when a more gradual increase in training load is better. As well as avoiding sudden increases in intensity or duration of training you should also avoid major changes in your cycling position. Seat height is important as it may influence muscle activity at the knee and any adjustments should be made gradually – no more than one centimetre per week. Longer crankshafts improve efficiency and power generation in theory, but they also offer greater resistance with each pedal revolution. Longer cranks create more stress with each pedal stroke, and thus are more inclined to cause knee pain.

Your choice of pedals may have a significant effect on your knees because your foot position alters naturally throughout the pedal revolution. With some clipless pedals the foot is held rigidly and compensates by deflecting movement further up the leg, which may cause maltracking at the knee. Clipless pedals emphasise any anatomical anomaly or biomechanical misalignment. Despite the fact that manufacturers have increased the amount of movement in the pedals, it is only on a lateral plane whereas natural foot movements occur in all directions. Clipless pedals are to be avoided if they cause knee pain. However this doesn't seem to be a problem for most people.

Muscle imbalance may give rise to patella maltracking. The most important muscle is on the inside, or medial side, of the thigh, and is a component of the quadriceps known as vastus medialis obliquus. Unfortunately this particular muscle is very prone to wasting, the medical term for weakening, which occurs very early in any knee injury. When returning to training, try to retrain this muscle in particular to help prevent further long-term knee pain. Traditional weight training exercises such as squats and leg extension exercises are of minimal

benefit as vastus medialis obliquus is only used in the last 15° of extension or the last part of the leg straightening. The appropriate static exercises known as Quads Drill are best demonstrated by a physiotherapist.

In cases of less severe knee pain you can continue to train on the bike but with some modifications to your technique: lower the saddle, cycle only on the level, at high cadence with no excess stress. Climbing inevitably means a lower cadence with greatly increased forces on the kneecap, so avoid climbing. If you have introduced extra long cranks then go back to your old ones. If you ride with cleats then go back to clips and straps, perhaps even without shoe plates so that your foot can adjust freely to its natural position. Stay off your knees as much as possible – if you are a plumber or electrician (or clergyman) this may be difficult – leave the gardening or carpet laying to someone else.

Anti-inflammatory medication will reduce inflammation at the back of the kneecap but only cures the symptoms and not the cause of the problem. Surgery is the last resort. The time spent in surgery, recovery, and rehabilitation may be longer than if you simply let the knee recover by rest, and gradually returning to training following the guidelines outlined above. Knee pain is not a pain to be suffered: if ignored it will only get worse. Treat it with respect.

Numbness and weakness of fingers can be caused while riding over an uneven surface, especially with the hands on the drops. A tight grip causes pressure on the heel of the hand, which may in turn cause bruising to a small nerve called the ulnar nerve. Normally this nerve gives sensation to part of the ring finger, little finger and movement to the finger muscles. When it is bruised it causes numbness and finger weakness known as cyclist's palsy. The numbness often eases some hours after the cycle ride but you should not return to cycling until it has gone completely. There may be other factors which trigger the condition, such as the position of the hands on the drops, pressure and vibration. A poorly fitted bike frame with a top tube that's too long for the rider will force him to lean forward putting pressure on the hands.

The condition is more common amongst inexperienced riders who grip tightly to control the bike, especially on rough terrain. Professional cyclists commonly pad their handlebars during difficult races over cobblestones, which not only reduces vibration, but also allows the cyclist to grip the bars without injuring the nerve. As a triathlete you can help prevent the condition by changing your hand position frequently during a race or training, by wearing well-padded cycling gloves, and using padded handlebars.

Another common hand injury is damage to the palms. During a crash it is a natural reaction to put out your hands to break a fall, rendering the palms vulnerable to severe friction injuries. The injury may heal with scar tissue, which is not as supple as normal skin, leading to disabling contractures which may require surgery at a later date. The best way to protect yourself is to wear proper cycling mitts with reinforced leather palms.

Fracture of the collar-bone or clavicle is a common occurrence. The clavicle is a relatively unimportant bone whose main purpose is to keep your shoulders apart. The contours of the bone may be felt just under the skin between the neck and shoulder. When falling off a bike at 25mph the arm can be driven up against the shoulder, pushing it against the collar-bone. If the bone is broken it will be too painful to move, let alone get back on the bike, and the cyclist will usually be taken to hospital for X-ray.

With most other fractures the bone is immobilised, but because of its relatively unimportant structural role and the small load it bears, it is not essential to completely immobilise the collar-bone for recovery. The usual treatment after X-ray diagnosis is to wear a sling, take pain relief medication and leave the fracture to heal. The two broken ends of the bone often do not meet perfectly and the athlete will be left with a step or bump along the contour of the bone.

Recovery takes about six weeks. For two weeks, while the ends of the bone are just beginning to knit, the shoulder will be too painful to do much movement. After a further two weeks the bone will have some stability, and as the break heals with fibrous tissue and gristle you may return to training using a turbo trainer. As healing progresses, the shoulder will become less painful, more stable, and it will be possible to cycle on flat well-surfaced roads. Any uneven surface will cause jarring and pain. In four to six weeks, you should be able to resume normal cycling. At this point the collar-bone will still be weak and could be easily injured again. Returning to running may take another two weeks, and the shoulder movement in swimming is affected for slightly longer still.

Overtraining

Swimming, cycling and running are endurance sports for which you will train long and hard. It is easy to be tempted to mimic the high training loads of the specialist for each sport. However this would almost certainly lead to overloading and overtraining.

In normal training, the body responds by adapting to cope efficiently with the training load. Overload means stressing the body with more work; this extra loading stimulates improvement. The load can be increased by adding distance or speed, and the body will adapt and then remain at that level until the load is increased again. When the body is allowed to recover it copes more easily with the increased loads of distance and speed.

The intensity and duration of the load, and time allowed for recovery are equally important. If the load is excessive or recovery inadequate the training effect is lost because the body is unable to adapt. If load and recovery remain unbalanced the body breaks down; at this point there is no physiological improvement and performance is impaired. This is the phenomenon known as overtraining. To avoid it you should monitor both load and recovery.

A good training principle is that the load should not be increased by increments greater than 10% per week. This applies to both speed and distance. Recovery means rest, both physical and psychological, allowing the body to recover from the previous load and prepare for the next. Overload and recovery form the foundation for all training programmes but the key to improvement lies in finding the right balance between appropriate load and recovery. One added complication is that we are all different: your programme must be tailored to you.

Tailor your training programme to your ability, strengths and weaknesses. There are other factors which can affect your performance: life events such as exams, personal stress and work problems. Training loads must not be seen in isolation but adjusted according to your needs. Performance must be seen in the context of job, lifestyle and workload. If you work hard every day and train in the evening you cannot expect to maintain the same workload as the full-time athlete who trains for three hours and has the remainder of the day to recover. The most important psychological determinant of performance is enthusiasm and keeness to train. If for any reason your enthusiasm is missing, your performance will be reduced.

Diet and lifestyle may also affect performance. If your diet is not adequate you cannot expect to maintain a suitable training programme. While a hectic social life will take its toll, constant training and racing, early nights and rigorous discipline could lead to a life of drudgery. Balance is important and finding the perfect formula, the ideal combination of work, training and play is the key to improving your performance.

Preventing overtraining

The best way to avoid the overtraining syndrome is to monitor your performance. One way is to measure your resting heart rate. Many of us are aware of pulse rate monitoring in physiological assessment and of the relationship between resting heart rate and fitness, but monitoring your resting pulse rate may also act as a guide to general well-being.

Take your pulse rate first thing in the morning before getting out of bed. Make a note of it. If for any reason there is a rise in the rate of about three beats per minute, then think about what caused it. Are you overtired? have you been training excessively? Could something else have affected you?

If during a period of heavy training, you don't feel quite so enthusiastic for the sport and simply cannot face it, this is a classic symptom of overtraining or staleness. A general loss of interest in life, work, family, hobbies and excessive tiredness also reflect overtraining syndrome. Loss of libido, or sex drive, is another recognised feature of overtraining. Not many athletes report it to their doctor.

Treatment

The treatment for overtraining is rest. If you neglect the recovery stage in your training programme, your performance will spiral downwards: keen athletes will train harder when they think their performance has slipped, but the appropriate response would be to rest. Overtraining is more likely to occur in determined, conscientious athletes who usually fail to see what is happening. In the early stages rest and recovery require a reduction in training load. Psychological rest may be aided by a change in the type of training or terrain; for example, if you regularly go out on your own, try training with a club, or if your programme includes a lot of interval training then try to do a more relaxed aerobic programme. Sometimes, the only option is complete rest. The temptation to interrupt a period of rest may be overwhelming, but if you want to break free of the overtraining syndrome you must guard against a premature return to a full training programme.

Through triathlon you'll form friendships that are as enduring as the sport itself. When the winner sticks around to salute you as you cross the line – as did Alison Hamilton after winning the Bath Triathlon – you'll know you are in good sporting company

CHAPTER 13

Mental preparation

There are some triathletes who lose races before they even line up for the swim. These are the same people who go through life saying a glass is half empty when they could say it's half full. They are the people who when faced with a task say, 'No can do,' instead of 'I know I can do it.'

Part of your success as a triathlete depends on your attitude, and to make the most of your potential you need a positive mental attitude. Mental preparation isn't just something you do the night before a triathlon: it's something that is on-going in day to day life. A negative mental attitude means you get to the start of a triathlon and tell your rivals how you didn't sleep the night before, how you twisted your ankle during your last interval session, how you haven't had as much training as you'd have liked. When the hard part comes later in the race, those nagging negative thoughts will return to the forefront of your mind. And

when a more positively focused athlete goes past you – perhaps the same athlete to whom you divulged your innermost, negative thoughts before the race – they're going to be able to play on your lack of positive thinking.

A positive attitude to life means that you are prepared to dig deep into yourself. It means that you are prepared to take on things that those less positive than you would let pass them by. If you are one of life's positive beings you will achieve more, have a richer life, even have a lot more anecdotes to recount to your friends than the man or woman who doesn't have any goals in life.

You don't need to tell the world what your goals are, but do admit them to yourself – you can even write them down. Remember, winning is relative. It could mean crossing the line first, or it could simply mean getting to the finish line. Winning is synonymous with achievement.

Name: **Date:**

Priority	Goal	Hurdles	Action	Started D/M/Y	Success D/M/Y

You may have been conditioned to think that it isn't the winning, but the taking part that matters. Winning, or achieving your goals, is important, and you should try always to give yourself the best chance of winning. That means preparing in the best possible way: prepare your bike, your kit, your body – and your mind.

Goal Setting

In thinking about what you want to achieve it helps to set yourself, lifetime, three-year, one-year, and one-month goals. It might help to limit yourself to a maximum of three per category – otherwise it's easy to get over

ambitious. Your monthly or short-term goals can be more numerous. Note down your goals in the table above.

Your lifetime goals should be quite general: for example you might simply want to live to a ripe old age. You will need a more definite plan to get there and the three-year, one-year, and one-month goals will be specific steps to help you to achieve that. You might decide to cut fatty foods out of your diet over the next month, to stop drinking coffee within a year and to build up an exercise programme that sees you fit enough to do the Ironman in three years.

Once you've listed your goals you need to evelute them in terms of importance. Evaluate your priorities. Give any three of your goals an A rating, signifying that they are the most important or urgent on your list. Give another three a B rating, meaning that they are of moderate urgency or importance. Give the rest a C rating. Jot down the ratings under the Priority column in the table.

Now decide how you will tackle your goals, starting with the A priorities. Think about the obstacles that will get in your way and how you will overcome them. Note your thoughts. Remember that the action you take to achieve your goal is likely to be a series of steps that will progressively bring you nearer to realising your goal. Your action list for A and B priorities should be implemented in one week if they concern a one-month goal, in two weeks if a one-year goal and in one month if a three-year goal. Note the dates on which you start to implement the action steps . . . and remember that there are deadlines.

Re-evaluate your goals and actions regularly – perhaps fortnightly. Note your achievements in the column headed Success. You might want to note down whether you followed your original plan of action or whether you had to improvise, and whether you were successful. If you haven't yet implemented a certain piece of action, re-evaluate the importance of the goal and work on it during the new fortnightly period.

Fear, the enemy

One of your biggest enemies in any challenging situation is fear. One definition of fear recognised by athletes is: False Expectations Appearing Real. How we perceive a situation affects our approach to it. Fear places problems in front of you, and when you manage to overcome those problems, you overcome a particular fear.

One way to master your fear of a given situation is to reduce the problems it poses. Ask yourself, on a scale of one to ten, how frightened you are of a situation. How frightened are you of finishing the swim in your first triathlon, or of completing the entire 112 miles of the Ironman's bike section? On a scale of one to ten, the answer could be 11. But you can reduce the problem, and thereby reduce the fear. Instead of thinking about the swim or the bike ride in its entirety, break it down into

components. Are you capable of swimming to that first buoy, just 800 metres from the shore? Can you get out of the transition area and past the first three mile markers on the bike within 20 minutes? The answer to both is probably yes. And, on a scale of one to ten, your fear quotient for both points might only be five.

Reduce problems and fears into components that you know you are capable of achieving, and offer yourself rewards when you achieve your individual targets. For example, you can break down the run of a triathlon into sections based on the aid stations. Each time you reach an aid station, reward yourself: have a banana, pour some cool water over your head, drink something.

Visualisation

Visualisation techniques are also a useful tool in mental preparation. They are like rehearsals to an actor, and they also train your neuromuscular facility, ie visualisation is thought to help your brain to send the right messages to your muscles.

Try the following exercises:

Perfect performance visualisation See in your mind how swimming, biking and running are performed using perfect style. Let the star actor in your mental rehearsal be you. What you are trying to do is train your mind to think about performing in the correct fashion. Often during races or training

Pre-race fear has many
ways of manifesting
itself

sessions, we go onto automatic pilot, and it would be helpful if automatic pilot incorporated perfect technique.

Visualise yourself running with the characteristics of, say, Liz McColgan; cycling with the grace of Gianni Bugno; swimming with the power and technique of Matt Biondi. In your visualisation, invest yourself with the effortless ease that these athletes seem to have even at maximum exertion. You could, if you prefer, visualise yourself as an animal or machine – as a gazelle when you're running, as Concorde on the bike, as a dolphin in the water.

Pre-race visualisation Mentally visualise the swim, bike and run courses, as well as your access from each to the transition area. Visualise yourself performing on the course and dealing with any difficulties that might occur: high winds, heavy rain, gravel on the cycle route. At all times during your visualisation, imagine that you are strong, positive and able to achieve your goals.

To help your pre-race visualisation, acquaint yourself with the course before the race. Know where and how steep or long the course's obstacles are, and then visualise how you will tackle them. Learn where the drinks stations are so that you can use them effectively during the race. Visualise feeling strong as you go through the penultimate drinks station, attacking and overtaking your biggest rival.

Acquainting yourself with a course is also helpful in that it will let you know if you need any special equipment during the race. Anti-glare goggles? An extra drinks bottle? Gears to help you climb, or gears that will allow you to hammer the flat?

Concentrate on the race's minor details during your pre-race visualisation: think about swimming in someone's slipstream, about sighting on the buoys, about handing in your swim cap, if you have to, at the end of the swim. Imagine the climbs on the bike and, more importantly perhaps, the descents. By knowing where and how long a race's descents are, you can win yourself a lot of time during the race. Preview the points on the run where you might be able to accelerate and pass someone. Remember: during your visualisation you're always swimming like a dolphin, climbing like Bugno and running with the ease and form of Liz McColgan.

Post-race visualisation This is like an action replay of the race. Look at the points in the race that went well for you, as well as those where you made mistakes. Try to evaluate why you went wrong, and then edit out those parts. In the end, you will be left with the perfect, visualised race.

If for example, you died on the run during a triathlon, visualise the race differently, ie with you finishing strongly on the run. Then, think about how you can achieve that. You might need to do training sessions that have you accelerating at the end of a long run. Recognise the changes that need to be made to correct your shortcomings, and then make them. You will learn more from the races at which you fail than those at which you succeed.

Try to include in your visualisations minor details that you would encounter in real life. Smell the chlorine of the swimming pool; feel the moist air; imagine yourself getting into the water, and how it surrounds you with its coolness. Visualise from within yourself, not looking down on yourself as an outsider.

Visualise yourself in real time, ie not in slow motion. If you were to conduct your visualisation sessions in slow motion, you would be training your brain cells to react slowly, to learn to switch into automatic pilot at a reduced speed. Obviously, that isn't what you are aiming at in a race.

You don't need a lot of time for a visualisation session. Take about five minutes to relax beforehand and then another five minutes to visualise. You can even visualise on the bus on the way to work, but you run the risk of missing your stop.

You have probably heard or read stories about people who have achieved physical tasks that normally would be far beyond their ability. They were able to achieve the seemingly impossible because they had the will to do so. On the other hand, with even perfect physical preparation, if the mind says 'no', the body will probably agree with it.

Hawaiian Crunch
Sarah on the right mental stuff

In the 1987 Ironman race, I had gone to Hawaii with the knowledge that I had been fifth in my last outing there. I wanted to finish in the top five that year, too, but there was some really tough competition. I looked at the starting list and saw at least ten names who would give me a good battle. Still, I knew what I had come out to Hawaii to achieve.

From the ninth mile on the run, I was battling it out with Amy Aikman, a pint-sized Texan competing in her first Ironman. She was a much faster natural runner than me, but she would stop and walk the aid stations, which occur every mile. I would go past her there, and then she would pass me again on the way to the next aid station.

She went away from me and then I saw her at the turn-around point. She wasn't very far in front of me, and so I was able to catch and pass her again. The see-sawing recommenced, until Amy pulled away again. That put her in fifth place and me in sixth.

I ran along with a little devil in my head, telling me, 'Well, sixth place isn't that bad.

In fact, it's very respectable.' But there was another voice inside me, reminding me that I had come to Hawaii to finish at least fifth. Amy was only 200 metres in front of me, and if I dug deep, I could take it.

There were five miles to go. I had, building up to the Ironman, done training sessions where I had run steadily for two and a half hours and then stepped on the accelerator and absolutely flown for the last five miles. That was what I had to do now. I had to dig in.

At that stage, someone in the crowd yelled, 'Come on, you can catch her. Fifth place is waiting for you up there.' I think they might also have yelled that there was an extra $1000 if I took fifth, and – yes – that thought did help a bit.

I went for it. There's a hill, about one and a half miles before the finish line of the Ironman, and I treated the top of the hill as the finish line. Once I got there, the rest was almost all downhill. I knew I could hold onto fifth place, and I did. It's one of those little ironies that you often find in triathlon that I passed Amy at the very place where Mark Allen broke away from Dave Scott two years later.

I had preconditioned myself for that race. I had set my goal to be fifth at least. If you prepare yourself to dig deep to achieve your goals, then when the crunch comes, you should be able to do so.

When you go through your mental preparations for a race, don't imagine yourself in slow-motion but at real speed, running strongly

CHAPTER 14

Time management

There is a saying that goes: if you want something done, ask a busy person. Maybe that adage should be updated to read: if you want something done, ask a triathlete.

As a triathlete, you cannot live in a training vacuum. The effort you put into getting yourself to the start line of a race should not override the effort that goes into being part of the human race. Even professional triathletes have to think about things other than tumble-turns and interval training. Day to day life is not going to slow down and wait for you when you go out on a 50-mile bike ride. You have to learn to arrange your life so that it, and your training programme can co-exist. You have to learn the art of time management.

Good time management starts with goal-setting. Before you can decide how to juggle the 24 hours in a day, you have to understand what you want to achieve in those 24 hours, and what

commitments you have that inevitably erode the amount of time available. To become a successful time manager, you need to:

1 Identify your goals. Write down your athletic and family goals for the coming year, for the next three years and for your lifetime. Pin those that relate to the coming year to the fridge door or carry them in your wallet – keep them somewhere where you are reminded of them daily.

2 Prioritise your goals. When you don't have enough time to achieve all that you want, you can at least set about achieving what you want most.

3 Be realistic. If you have difficulty breaking eight minutes for a running mile now, don't expect to be Roger Bannister in a week.

4 Include your commitments to family and close friends in your goal setting.

5 Don't forget your personal day-to-day

At age 35 Mark Allen ran to his tenth victory in the Nice Triathlon. Up until three kilometres to go to the finish line, he was in the able company of Simon Lessing, but Allen's experience paid dividends

Needs and commitments when setting your goals. This includes your job, the washing and ironing, as well as your training.

Having identified your yearly, three-yearly and lifetime goals, make monthly goals. These will remind you how you aim to progress toward your longer term goals. They break down further into what you want to do in the coming week, and during the next 24 hours. Make a list of these immediate-

MONTHLY PROGRAM SHEET							
Name:				Date:			
Monday	Tuesday	Wednesday	Thursday	Friday	Saturday	Sunday	Date

Fill in this table with what you would like to achieve

MONTHLY SCHEDULE

	Swim	Bike	Run	Weights	Stretching	Mental Rehearsal	Competitions
January							
February							
March							
April							
May							
June							
July							
August							
September							
October							
November							
December							

PERSONAL BESTS

SWIM		
	50 m	25 m
	100 m	200 m
	400 m	1000 m
	800 m	1500 m
	1 mile	2000 m
	2 miles	3000 m
	2.4 miles	4000 m

BIKE	
	5 miles
	10 miles
	25 miles
	50 miles
	100 miles
	112 miles

RUN		
	6 miles	100 m
	10 km	200 m
	10 miles	400 m
	20 km	800 m
	½ marathon	1000 m
	20 miles	1500 m
	Marathon	1 mile
		3000 m
		5000 m

In this table, note down what you actually do achieve

term goals. Revise the list daily, dealing with items as they arise and crossing them off the list as you achieve them.

Only when you know what your goals are can you think about managing them effectively. A good manager aims to expend minimum effort for maximum effect. Compare time management to swimming: you create propulsion but you're slowed by drag. In life, there are things that motivate you, that propel you forward, that compel you to achieve. At the

WEEKLY PROGRAM SHEET

Week
Aim: **PREPARE IRONMAN**

Week ending:

Week No.: **38**

Keep a weekly program sheet. Monday's example is from Sarah Springman's Ironman preparation

Day	Weather	Sleep	Heart Rate / Wt	Session	Time	Activity	Description	Intensity >85%	Intensity 70-85	Intensity <70%	Total	Time	Cals spent
Monday	fine bldy day	7	40		6.30	Swim Stretch bike	easy 6 x 500 / Swim x 2 recovery			3000 10	3000 10	7510 40	
Tuesday													
Wednesday													
Thursday													
Friday													
Saturday													
Sunday													

Total Sleep	~	Assessment of Aims			S %				
					B %				
Body Fat/ Weight +/–					R %				
					Weights/circuits/aerobics/other				
Illness/ Injury					Yoga/stretching				
					Mental Rehearsal				

Total:

same time, other elements nag away at you and try to slow you down.

To make the most of the time you have for triathlon training, you need to minimise the negative factors. A good way to start is by communicating effectively with people around you. Make absolutely certain that everyone

knows what you want to do and what is important to you. Then, when you go out to do a training session, you'll be able to do it without worrying about the little bits and pieces that nag at you.

Balance the time available to you with a training programme that you are

Learning to manage
your time well will help
you get across the line
early

capable of following and which permits
you to maximise your potential as a
triathlete. In terms of hours in the day,
you might be able to swim every
morning of the week from seven to
eight am. But, if training daily before
work leaves you too tired to do
anything else, then your morning
training sessions are not an effective
use of time.

If you have to travel often, find out
in advance from people who know the
place that you'll be visiting where you
can swim, bike and run while there. If
you can't take your bike with you, ask
if there is a gym that you can use, and
do anaerobic threshold sessions on the
exercise bikes. Do a little homework in
advance so that you can arrive
prepared and ready to take advantage
of any training opportunities that might
exist.

Plan in advance, make lists, refer to
the lists, cross things off, and
communicate. And be realistic, so that
you really can achieve a reasonable
percentage of the things that you set
out to. Don't expect to achieve
everything. A 60% achievement rate is
admirable.

An often overlooked but vital
element in a well-managed day is hours
of sleep. Sleep is a tool for combatting
stress, and top triathletes not only sleep
long hours each night, but also take
little catnaps during the day.

Stress attacks you daily, in varying
doses and from all directions. Training
is a form of stress; work is stressful.
Home life has its sources of stress;
emotional distress can be a powerful
demotivator. Any kind of stress will
knock you down and hold you back.
Make time in your day for dealing with
and recovering from stress: yoga,
stretching, a quiet walk perhaps. The
unwelcome and unexpected – a death,
divorce, forced move – can make the
simplest training run feel as hard as the
marathon at the end of the Ironman.
When these drag factors of life do afflict
you, don't be afraid to reassess your
goals, at least in the short-term.

Time is always of the essence to a
triathlete. Optimal use of time will help
you to achieve maximal impact.

CHAPTER 15

Competitor information

from the British Triathlon Association

1 General

The following rules are intended for the purpose of creating equal opportunity for all competitors and provide a basis for reasonable safety and protection in an atmosphere of sportsmanship and fair play. This implies that any competitor who commits an illegal act, whether an unfair advantage has been gained or not will be penalised.

1 Competitors must exercise sound, mature judgement, carry out all reasonable instructions from officials, obey the laws of the land and observe traffic regulations.

2 Competitors are ultimately responsible for their own safety and for the safety of others.

3 Competitors must take responsibility for knowing the rules and abiding by them.

4 It is the competitors responsibility to be properly prepared for an event and to ensure that their equipment is suitable and fit for its intended purpose.

2 Conduct

Competitors must conduct themselves in a proper manner and not bring the sport into disrepute. Infringement of any of the following carries a penalty of disqualification from the event and possible withdrawal of membership of the Association.

1 All other competitors, officials, volunteers and spectators must be treated with respect and courtesy.

2 Foul or abusive language is not permitted.

3 Standards of dress should be adequate as befits a public place – ie no nudity.

3 Membership and race licences

All competitors must be either a current member of the BTA and hold a

BTA race licence or be liable to pay an additional fee.

1 To be eligible to qualify for awards in National Championships a competitor must be a British National and hold a current race licence on the day of the event.

2 Teams in National Championships must be composed of BTA members of the same BTA affiliated club.

3 All persons wishing to participate in international events must have a current race licence with an international endorsement.

4 Entry to European and world championship events must be via the official BTA procedures.

5 In accordance with ETU rules, all age groups are determined by subtracting the year of birth from the year of the competition. ITU world championship races may vary in their method of determination of age groups – if in doubt contact BTA HQ.

6 BTA and ETU age groups for the year 1992 will be determined as follows:

Age	Category	Year of Birth
a	Juveniles	1979-80
c	Juniors	1973-75
e	Senior 2	1963-67
g	Senior 4	1953-57
i	Veteran 2	1943-47
k	Veteran 4	1933-37
m	Veteran 6	1923-27
p	Veteran 8	1913-17

Age	Category	Year of Birth
b	Youths	1976-78
d	Senior 1	1968-72
f	Senior 3	1958-62
h	Veteran 1	1948-52
j	Veteran 3	1938-42
l	Veteran 5	1928-32
n	Veteran 7	1918-22
q	Veteran 9	Pre 1913

7 Juveniles may only compete in events of less than the Olympic distance. Swim must be pool-based and the cycling and running sections must be on closed roads. Written parental consent to compete is required.

8 Youths may compete in events up to and including Olympic distance. Written parental consent to compete is required.

9 Juniors may compete in events up to and including middle distance.

10 Members may only compete for the club and region stated on their race licence within one subscription year.

4 Insurance

The membership fee includes an element to cover personal accident insurance which is valid whilst you are training, racing or travelling to or from an event. It also gives you cover against third party claims, eg if you crash into a shop window and the owner sues you for damages.

1 The BTA insurance policy does not cover you for losses due to damage or theft of your equipment. This may be covered on your own household contents insurance –

check and make arrangements if necessary. *NB many policies do not cover damage caused whilst racing unless you have declared your racing in advance.*

2 All events must be covered by adequate public liability, member to member, and third party insurance for the officials and volunteers as well as all those competing in the event. Such insurance is available at advantageous rates as part of the BTA's sanctioning procedure.

3 Competitors should be aware that unsanctioned events and non-members of the Association may not have any insurance cover. It is the policy of the Association both to discourage its members from taking part in unsanctioned events and to take steps to prevent such events from taking place on the public highway.

5 Entries

Members intending to compete should make enquiries and obtain entry forms as early as possible, always include an SAE.

1 Most events have an upper limit on the number of competitors, the earlier you enter the better your chances. Always try to enter at least one month in advance.

2 Any competitor using another's race entry will be disqualified from the competition. Never be tempted to take a friend's place in an event it can result in a wife and family being notified of an accident, them dashing 100 miles to a hospital and finding it was somebody else.

3 Members of the Association qualify for a reduced entry fee (£2.00) in all events.

Proof of membership may be requested either on the entry form or at registration.

6 Registration

It is vital that all participants attend any registration and race briefings prior to an event. In low key sprint races these may be held shortly before the start but at national championships and other major races they may be held on the afternoon or evening before a race. Make sure that you know when the briefing is and that you attend it.

1 It is at this time that any last minute details and/or changes will be presented, eg wetsuit regulations, roadworks in progress, number and positions of feed or water stations, etc.

2 Number markings will be carried out.

3 Bike and helmet checks may be carried out.

4 If you know that you will not be competing in an event that you have entered please make every effort to advise the organisers well in advance. It may mean that somebody else can be given a place where restrictions on numbers apply.

7 Race conduct

All competitors must wear any official swim cap, bib or number provided by the race organiser. It must be worn unaltered and be visible/readable at all times.

1 Competitors must be adequately clothed at all times, the minimum being a one or two piece non-transparent swimsuit together with a cycling or running top if appropriate. Male competitors must ensure that their upper body is clothed during the cycling and running sections of the event.

2 Individual's or club's sponsors names or logos may appear on clothing but it should be noted that special conditions and size limits apply to international kit. Members of national teams will be advised of their kit regulations by their team managers.

3 It is the responsibility of the competitor to know and follow the prescribed course in all three disciplines, however the Association's sanctioning procedures should ensure that all courses are clearly marked.

4 Competitors may not accept assistance in any form during an event except that which may be provided by the race organisers. This especially applies to members of the competitor's family and/or friends who may attempt to follow or lead and/or intercept or pace a rider or runner. Any such behaviour may result in the disqualification of that competitor.

8 Transition areas

In order to avoid accidents, safeguard equipment and protect your personal possessions, athletes should not attempt to bring helpers, friends or family members into any transition area.

1 Your equipment must be placed in its allotted space and not strewn around where it may hinder the progress of other competitors.

2 Your cycle must be placed in its correct position in the racks both at the start and finish of the cycle section.

3 You may only mount your cycle and start riding at the officially designated position. When you return you must dismount where indicated and walk or run with your bike to your allocated position.

9 Swimming

Any stroke may be used but in pool swims organisers have the discretion to restrict the use of butterfly, backstroke, tumble-turns or diving.

1 Standing or resting on the bottom or on a non-moving object is allowed but unfair advantage or progress must not be made and may result in disqualification.

2 In an emergency you should attempt to raise one arm overhead and call for assistance.

3 Wetsuits of a material no thicker than 5mm in any part and not covering the hands or feet may be worn when the water temperatures and swim length combinations below are not exceeded. They should be compulsory when the water temperature is less than 14°C. At temperatures below 11°C the swim should be cancelled.

Swim distance	Wetsuits forbidden
Less than 2000m	> = 21°C
2000 – 2999m	> = 22°C
3000m and over	> = 23°C

Organisers are requested to comply with the following recommendations regarding water temperature and maximum swim distances:

Water Temperature	Max swim length
13°C	2000m
12°C	1000m
11°C	500m
Below 11°C	No open water swimming

4 Swim caps goggles and nose clips may be used but flippers, leggings or any other aid are not allowed.

10 Cycling

All cycles used must be fit for the purpose and have two independent and efficiently working brakes when a freewheel is fitted.

1 Spot checks may be made on condition and road worthiness and you may be required to complete a self-certificate of checks that you have personally completed.

2 Disc wheels may only be used on the rear.

3 Cycle helmets approved to Snell Foundation or ANSI Z90.4 standard must be worn throughout the cycling section of an event. They must be fastened before mounting your bike and may not be unfastened and removed before you have dismounted. All approved helmets carry stickers on the inside – if in doubt check before purchase. No other form of helmet, eg leather hairnet, glass-fibre shell etc is allowed. Also elastic chin straps are unacceptable.

4 You must not ride your cycle in the transition area, a clearly defined mount/dismount line should be available.

5 Group riding or pacing (drafting) is not permitted (See Section 11).

6 No individual support vehicles are allowed.

7 Any competitor taking assistance or pace from vehicles driven by friends, helpers or family will be disqualified.

8 You may cover part of the course on foot if you prefer but you must push or carry your cycle in such circumstances.

9 Headsets such as the Sony Walkman must not be worn.

11 Drafting

Drafting or taking pace is not allowed during the cycling section of any event. It is an individual event and riders may not take pace from any other cyclist (competitor or not) or vehicle. Riders must be no closer than 7 metres (approx 5 bike lengths) measured from your front wheel to to the next competitor's rear wheel.

Side by side riding is only permitted during overtaking in which case the manoeuvre should be completed within 30 seconds. It is the responsibility of the overtaken rider to drop back as soon as the overtaking front wheel is level with your front wheel.

Draft busters will be instructed to show a yellow card and blow a whistle at any rider considered to be drafting. When this happens the rider must bring their cycle to a complete stop and place both feet on the ground. They may then restart with no further penalty (Rider's numbers will be noted and any rider stopped twice or more in the same event will be disqualified).

12 Running

No form of locomotion other than running or walking is permitted, ie you can't crawl to the line! No individual support by vehicle, cyclist or escort runners is allowed.

13 Appeals

Protests may be made against other competitors' conduct or decisions made by officials.

1 Appeals against penalties must be made within one hour of completing the course. They must be in writing and accompanied by a fee of £5.00 – refundable if the appeal is upheld.

2 At national championships and international races a race jury will consider appeals. In other cases appeals will be considered by the race referee.

14 Drugs

The taking of any form of performance-enhancing drug is not permitted. The use of *blood doping* is similarly banned. The Sports Council Drug Testing Unit will visit several events during each season and competitors must, if selected, provide urine or blood samples required for testing. Out of season testing also take place. Any refusal to participate in such testing will be considered equivalent to a positive finding. All athletes are reminded that the onus is upon them to have full knowledge of the rules concerning doping. Ignorance of the rules is not considered a defence.

Members should be aware that many familiar remedies available without prescription – especially those for colds and flu – contain banned substances. The two cases of positive drug tests in the UK were both found in athletes who had taken cold remedies in the week before a race. If in doubt you should consult the pharmacist and say that you require a remedy that does not contain banned substances (If you are that ill should you be racing at all?).

1 In the event of a positive test competitors will face the appropriate penalty as demanded by IOC and ITU regulations.

2 A list of any competitors found to test positive will be forwarded to the International Triathlon Union (ITU).

3 A list of banned substances is published separately together with appropriate medical guidelines.

The following guidelines have been prepared by a pharmacist who is also a practising triathlete. The IOC prohibits the use of substances grouped into various categories:

Doping substances

Stimulants Amphetamines, Cocaine, Ephedrine, Phenylpropanolamine, Pseudoephedrine
Narcotic analgesics Codeine, Morphine, Pethidine, Pentazocine
Anabolic steroids Nandrolone (Deca-durabolin), Stanozolol (Stromba), Testosterone, Oxandrolone
Diuretics Bendrofluazide, Frusemide (Lasix), Hydrochlorothiazide, spironolactone, triamterine

Substances subject to certain restrictions

Alcohol
Local anaethestics
Corticosteroids – banned except for topical use (ie skin ointments), inhalational therapy (ie nasal sprays), and local or intra-articular injections

Doping methods

Blood doping Erythropoietin (Recormon, Eprex) pharmacological, chemical and physical methods
Almost all of the above substances are available legally but only on prescription. Some are produced by several companies under different brand names, so if you obtain a prescription from your doctor or dentist you should ask the prescriber or the pharmacist whether the medicine is on the IOC banned list (take a copy of the list with you – it's in the BTA handbook). If you buy a medicine over the counter ask the pharmacist if it contains banned substances.

Permitted by the IOC:

Pain relief Paracetamol, Aspirin, Ibuprofen (Nurofen). Medicines made up of a mixture of ingredients including codeine eg Solpadeine, are not allowed.
Colds Otrivine drops or spray, steam or menthol inhalation, Paracetomol, Aspirin (do not use Actifed or Sudafed as they contain pseudoephedrine)
Cough Expectorants – Benylin chesty cough, Guanor, Covonia Supressants – Pholcodine linctus, Pavacol-D, Pholcomed (preparations containing codeine are not permitted)
Sore throat Merocets, Merocaine, Aspirin gargle, antibiotics (prescription only)
Hay fever Anti-histamines such as Triludan, Piriton, Aller-Eze (not Aller-Eze plus) Opticrom eye drops, Beconase, Syntaris
Vomiting Maxolon, Stemetil, Motilium, Stugeron, Dioralyte, Rehidrat
Diarrhoea Imodium, Arret, Kaopectate, Lomotil, Dioralyte, Rehidrat
Ginseng This can be a problem because some preparations contain the Chinese herb Ephedra which contains the banned substance pseudoephedrine

15 Penalties

Rule infringements will be signalled by the showing of either a yellow or red card, the blowing of a whistle, the calling of your number, or a combination of these.

1 On the showing of a yellow card the competitor must stop and take whatever action is needed to correct the problem.

2 If the problem is not corrected a red card will be shown, signifying disqualification. Competitors must then make their way back to the transition area and hand in their number.

3 In cases of drafting you must follow the 'two foot rule' as explained in section 11.

4 Certain infringements, eg riding without a helmet, riding without a vest/jersey, public nudity, carry immediate disqualification penalties in which case a red card will be shown. Competitors must then make their way back to the transition area and hand in their number.

16 Awards

There will be awards ceremonies at all national championships with the following presentations made:

Medals to

open category	1st 2nd and 3rd	male and female
Age groups D-Q	1st	male and female

Certificates will be presented to 2nd and 3rd places (male and female) in age groups D-Q. Juniors, Youths and Juveniles (age group C-A) will have their own championship events. The previous policy of moving athletes into a younger age group if there are fewer than five competing is to be withdrawn for both males and females. From 1993 onwards a minimum prize purse of £1,000 is to be recommended for all national championships. Please do your best to be present at all awards ceremonies – it might be you up there one day!

Useful addresses

British Triathlon Association, Dover Leisure Centre, Townwall Road, Dover

International Triathlon Union, 1154 West 24th Street, North Vancouver, BC V7P 2J2, Canada

European Triathlon Union, Didier Lehaneff, 13 Rue Massenet, 93270 Sevran, France

Sports Council, Information Centre, 16 Upper Woburn Place, London WC1H 0QP

Scottish Sports Council, Caledonia House, South Gyle, Edinburgh EH12 9DQ

Sports Council for Northern Ireland, House of Sport, Upper Malone Road, Belfast BT9 5LA

Sports Council for Wales, National Sports Centre for Wales, Sophia Gardens, Cardiff CF1 9SW

Index